Mother's Milk and Male Fantasy
in Nineteenth-Century French Narrative

Studies in Modern and Contemporary France   9

Studies in Modern and Contemporary France

Series Editors

Assistant Professor Siham Bouamer, Sam Houston State University
Professor Denis M. Provencher, University of Arizona
Professor Martin O'Shaughnessy, Nottingham Trent University

The Studies in Modern and Contemporary France book series is a new collaboration between the Association for the Study of Modern and Contemporary France (ASMCF) and Liverpool University Press (LUP). Submissions are encouraged focusing on French politics, history, society, media and culture. The series will serve as an important focus for all those whose engagement with France is not restricted to the more classically literary, and can be seen as a long-form companion to the Association's journal, *Modern and Contemporary France,* and to *Contemporary French Civilization*, published by Liverpool University Press.

Mother's Milk and Male Fantasy in Nineteenth-Century French Narrative

LISA ALGAZI MARCUS

Liverpool University Press

First published 2022 by
Liverpool University Press
4 Cambridge Street
Liverpool
L69 7ZU

This paperback edition published 2024

British Library Cataloguing-in-Publication data
A British Library CIP record is available

ISBN 978-1-80207-008-8 (hardback)
ISBN 978-1-83553-717-6 (paperback)

Typeset by Carnegie Book Production, Lancaster
Printed and bound by CPI Group (UK) Ltd, Croydon CR0 4YY

Contents

Acknowledgments

So many people have supported me over the years as I have worked to bring this project to fruition that I'm not sure I can name them all here. First, let me thank the Beneficial Hodson Trust, Hood College, and the Hood College Board of Associates for the funding I have received for sabbatical research and summer travel to consult archival sources in France. I must also thank the lovely staff and directors of the *Musée des Nourrices et des Enfants de L'Assistance Publique* in the tiny village of Alligny-en-Morvan, France, particularly Martine Chalandre, Jean-Pierre Cortet, and Elise Armand, who very graciously spent a day in October 2017 showing me the museum's archives and sharing stories of the history of wet-nursing in their community. I am extremely grateful for their assistance.

Many colleagues have supported me in this endeavor, including Allan Pasco, who offered recommendations and advice at multiple points and whose work on nursing mothers in Romantic literature formed the foundation for a large part of this book, and my dear friends Mary Jane Cowles, Annie Smart, Ione Crummy, and Susie Hennessy, who have heard countless iterations of this project over the years and who have pulled me out of the research doldrums more than once. Thanks to Mary Jane Cowles for the suggestion that became the new title of this book! I'm grateful to all the colleagues from NCFS, too numerous to name, who have sent me random breast-feeding references, and to Sayeeda Mamoon for her generous review. Similarly, my colleagues and closest friends, Emilie Amt, Amy Gottfried, Karen Hoffman, and Jenni Ross, have been stalwart supporters through the years, helping me to overcome obstacles and accomplish my goals. I am indebted to them all.

Last, but far from least, my deepest thanks to my wonderful husband David and my two children, Alyx and Charlie, all of whom have entered my life since I started work on this project. Their love, encouragement, and baked goods have made the hard times easier and the good times a lot more fun. Love y'all!

Introduction

In the midst of writing my doctoral dissertation on maternal subjectivity in the works of Stendhal, thirty years ago, I came across an intriguingly erotic portrayal of breast-feeding in Balzac's *Memoirs of Two Young Married Women*. Many years later, after publishing my first book and giving birth to two children, I returned to this topic with the goal of identifying trends in the representation of breast-feeding throughout the nineteenth century in France. I started with these questions: How did the representation of breast-feeding in French literature and popular culture evolve from the Revolutionary period to 1900, and what was the relationship between representation and reality? In other words, did the literary portrayals of breast-feeding women reflect real experience as lived by French women of the time, or rather contemporary authors' views of the ideal mother? The answers to these questions are necessarily grounded in historical and cultural context. A number of seminal socio-historical studies on breast-feeding history in France were published in the 1970s and 1980s, including Carol Duncan's "Happy Mothers" (1979), Fanny Fay-Sallois's *Les Nourrices à Paris au XIXe siècle* (1980), and George Sussman's 1982 book *Selling Mothers' Milk: The Wet-Nursing Business in France, 1715–1914*. Although Mary Jacobus's *First Things: The Maternal Imaginary in Literature, Art and Psychoanalysis* (1995) and Marilyn Yalom's *The History of the Breast* (1997) offered a glance at maternal imagery through multiple cultures and time periods, their treatment of France concentrated primarily on the eighteenth century, particularly the political iconography of the Revolutionary period. Chapter 1 consists of a socio-historical overview of breast-feeding in eighteenth-century France, which provides the framework for an examination of trends after 1800.

While the works listed above mentioned literary texts in passing, few scholars to date have done a more thorough analysis of the portrayal of breast-feeding in French literature and popular culture in the nineteenth century. Gal Ventura's 2018 book, *Maternal Breast-Feeding and Its Substitutes in Nineteenth-Century French Art*, was the first scholarly work to focus on the topic but limited its scope primarily to the visual arts. Despite a smattering of articles on breast-feeding in nineteenth-century literature in the 1980s and 1990s in the works of Émile Zola, no one has yet done for literature what Ventura did so skillfully for the visual arts. My goal in this book is to bridge this gap by providing a narrative overview of breast-feeding representations in literature throughout nineteenth-century France, from the turn of the century to 1899.

In her introduction, Ventura refers to anthropologist Brigitte Jordan's assertion that breast-feeding, as a cultural signifier of motherhood, is shaped by its socio-historical context (Ventura, 2018, xiii). I begin by examining the representation of breast-feeding in nineteenth-century France, in literature as well as in popular culture, in light of the unique history of post-revolutionary France and its ramifications for gender roles. The tension between the authentic lived experience of breast-feeding French women during this period and their representation in cultural artifacts such as literature and art lies at the heart of my project, complicated further by the fact that the producers of these artifacts were primarily male.

As I collected and analyzed literary examples of breast-feeding, I slowly came to realize the answer to my original question. In most cases, literary portrayals of the act of breast-feeding in French literature during the nineteenth century had very little to do with real life and everything to do with the imaginations, hopes, and desires of the authors who created them. Whether those hopes stemmed from political beliefs or unmet psychological or sexual desires, seldom were they grounded in real-life observation. The authors of these texts have one thing in common: a lack of first-hand experience with the act of breast-feeding children. While these authors were mostly men, at least one woman, Marceline Desbordes-Valmore, wrote of the maternal breast in the same symbolic and idealized fashion as her Romantic male contemporaries, after sending her own children to wet nurses, as most

Frenchwomen did in those days (Descaves, 1910, 90). The one notable exception is George Sand, who left ample documentation through her correspondence of her experience of nursing her own children, an experience that clearly informed the matter-of-fact accounts of breast-feeding in her novels (Sand, 1964, 108).

From the beginning of my research, I identified some overarching trends in nineteenth-century breast-feeding representations. During the first decades of the century, there seems to be a relative dearth of portrayals of nursing mothers in literature, which is even more striking due to the contrast with the plethora of such images in the final years of the previous century. In Chapter 2, I outline the possible reasons for this change, building on the foundation of Allan Pasco's influential work, *Sick Heroes: French Society and Literature in the Romantic Age, 1750–1850.* Through an analysis of the few instances of breast-feeding in Romantic literature, I show that those representations tell us less about the real embodied experiences of women and more about the hopes and fears of male Romantic authors, most of whom were raised not by their own mothers, but by hired wet nurses. Deprived of the bonding experience with their mothers, these authors tended to write of the maternal breast, whether absent or present, only to highlight its significance in the development of the male protagonist at the center of most Romantic narratives.

In Chapter 3, I will take a closer look at the topic that first caught my attention: the eroticization of breast-feeding in realist and naturalist French fiction, from Balzac to Zola. While the sexualization of the maternal breast in France can be traced back through the centuries, with an early example being Dr. Laurent Joubert's medical treatises in the late 1500s, its literary representation seems particularly well-suited to the comprehensive history of contemporary life that realist fiction in general, such as Balzac's body of fictional works known as the *Human Comedy,* purported to encompass. The naturalist writings of Zola and his followers, with their literary experimentation and social commentary, continued this trend, often featuring breast-feeding women in both positive and negative lights. However, once again, the women we see in such works are often products, not of objective observation or embodied female experience, but rather of the psyches of a generation of male authors. We will see how breast-feeding became a symbol of either the quintessential good mother, as in Balzac's *Memoirs of Two Young Married Women,* or the proverbial evil stepmother/wet nurse in Alexandre Hepp's novel *Another's Milk*. The maternal breast as sexual object thus serves a twin purpose of redemption and revulsion, fascination and rejection.

Finally, in Chapter 4, I will examine the political implications of the figure of Marianne during the Third Republic. The bare-breasted, often breast-feeding, female-bodied allegory of Liberty or the Republic that replaced symbols of the French monarchy after the Revolution in 1789 returned to prominence in the latter half of the nineteenth century, acquiring the name Marianne sometime after the fall of the Second Republic. After an overview of Marianne as a political icon of both the Second and Third Republics, I will analyze two literary representations of nursing women called Marianne in the late nineteenth century, one positive and one negative, and their symbolic significance in the authors' conception of republican ideals in the highly politicized climate of the turn of the century.

Chapter 1

Nursing Mothers
in Eighteenth-Century France
The Personal is Political

The eighteenth century in France saw an abundance of maternal representations in both literature and the fine arts, particularly in the decades following the publication of Rousseau's immensely popular novel, *Julie, or the New Heloise*, in 1761. Mothers were portrayed in a variety of attitudes and occupations, including breast-feeding, that quintessential maternal obligation, according to Rousseau. To quote his immortal words on the subject in *Emile, or on Education*, published in 1762:

> She who breast-feeds another's child instead of her own is a bad mother; how could she be a good wet nurse? [...] But if mothers would deign to breast-feed their children, morals would reform themselves, the feelings of nature would awaken in all hearts, and the State would be repopulated. (Rousseau, 1964, 18)[1]

For Rousseau, the refusal of mothers to breast-feed constituted the primary cause of the social problems of his time. The central position of maternal breast-feeding in Rousseau's social theory brought mothers a new prestige, along with a certain sense of responsibility for the welfare of future generations. It also placed maternal breast-feeding at the center of the political reforms that culminated in revolution, granting mothers a place in the construction of the new French nation. Although their role was confined to the private sphere, mothers remained essential to Rousseau's vision of socio-political reforms that would restore morality and revitalize the body politic.

While this insistence on breast-feeding as a primary maternal duty was far from new in the 1760s – it echoes the words of moralists and

medical authorities in France from at least the 1500s on – Rousseau
seems to have been significantly more successful than his predecessors
in convincing women of the importance of their role as mothers,
perhaps by emphasizing the sentimental benefits to the mother and
to the family unit. In spite of, or perhaps because of, his contention
that women belonged in the home, supporting their husbands and
raising their children, female readers adored Rousseau, referring to
him as "above other men" and taking Julie, eponymous heroine of his
novel, as "a model of all virtues."[2] Even Germaine Necker de Staël,
a well-known author and public figure, who clearly chose not to
follow Rousseau's teachings on women staying in the private sphere,
acknowledged the merits of his arguments in an early work entitled
Letters on Jean-Jacques Rousseau:

> Oh! Even though he wished to deprive women of some rights
> not natural to their sex, how well he granted them all the rights
> that have always been theirs! [...] even though he brought
> women down from a usurped throne, how well he restored them
> to the one Nature intended for them! (Staël, 1979, 47)[3]

According to Staël, Rousseau was entirely responsible for a rebirth of
maternal feelings "in a certain class of society; he made mothers aware
of this duty and this joy; he inspired in them the desire not to allow
others to steal the first caresses of their children" (1979, 47).[4] Staël even
went so far as to see this reclaiming of maternal responsibilities as a way
for some women to bring meaning to their lives: "[D]id he not teach
them to rediscover in their child a second youth, whose hope would
be reborn for them when their own youth was over? Oh! All is not
yet lost for the unhappy mother whose mistakes or whose destiny has
spoiled her life!" (56).[5]

Lesley Walker, in her book *A Mother's Love: Crafting Feminine Virtue
in Enlightenment France*, theorized that the maternal figure played
a critical role in the Enlightenment project of social and political
transformation for the common good. Walker analyzed "the role
of the mother as educator, supervisor, and moral center of a newly
conceived domestic space" that appeared in both literary and artistic
production by women in the eighteenth century (2008, 25). The
concept of the capable mother passing along vital knowledge to her
offspring, particularly her daughters, formed the basis for many of the
popular novels by eighteenth-century French women such as Stéphanie

de Genlis as well as the successful careers of painters such as Elisabeth Vigée Lebrun and Marguerite Gérard.

Following Rousseau's lead, in the late eighteenth century, well-known artists such as Greuze and Fragonard, as well as many lesser-known artists such as Louis-Roland Trinquesse and Jean-Laurent Mosnier,[6] created a host of images of young mothers with infants at their breasts. Greuze's drawing *The Beloved Mother* (*La Mère bien-aimée*), exhibited in the Paris Salon of 1765, shows a joyous woman inundated by the caresses of her numerous offspring, her breast exposed as though she has just nursed her youngest. As Walker and art historian Bernadette Fort have pointed out, Diderot and other contemporary critics remarked on the mother's ecstatic expression and its sexual connotations. In her analysis of this image, Fort emphasized the sexual nature of the breast-feeding experience: "In the finished painting, the overwhelmed, orgasmic expression of Greuze's *Beloved Mother* takes over the ideology of sexualized nursing and holds out to mothers the promise of a delicate sensual pleasure as an incentive to nursing" (2006, 129). This echoed the words of Dr. Laurent Joubert, who had described the sensual rewards of breast-feeding in 1578 (1578, 418). Walker suggested that the sexualized maternal figure in Greuze's image created discomfort in the viewers as it attempted to blend the concepts of passion and motherhood. According to Walker, "[w]hereas the success of Rousseau's novel [*La Nouvelle Héloïse*] can be attributed to the transformation of amorous passion into virtuous motherhood, Diderot's response to Greuze's painting demonstrates that this same tale in the hands of male painters did not work as seamlessly" (2008, 97). This tension between sexuality and virtuous motherhood was resolved in the visual arts by the work of female artists such as Elisabeth Vigée Lebrun and Marguerite Gérard, whose works typically excluded the father figure in a lyrical celebration of the mother–child bond.

Thanks to popular engravings of this and similar works (by Greuze and others), such images could be viewed and even owned by many people of various social milieu. Genre paintings showing happy nursing mothers abounded in France throughout the last four decades of the eighteenth century, increasing in number in the official artistic Salon in the 1780s and 1790s (Calley-Galitz, 1998, 25–35). The popularity of these images in the visual arts was echoed in literary works of the period. In the words of art historian Carol Duncan, "The joys of maternity became a fashionable literary theme, its every aspect eloquently told in prose and poetry, from the sensual rewards of breast-feeding to the unequaled pleasure of receiving a child's caresses and kisses" (1993, 19). Isabelle Brouard-Arends dedicated large sections of her book *Maternal Images and Lives in Eighteenth-Century French Literature* to textual representations of maternal breast-feeding, particularly in the works of women novelists from 1760 to 1790. In one example, *Zélie in the Desert*, by Madame Daubenton, breast-feeding is presented as not only a duty but a pleasure, bringing the loving couple closer together as well as facilitating the mother's recovery from childbirth: "I recovered quickly because I was nursing, and besides, I was content, happy, well cared for, and I was constantly the recipient of Monsieur d'Ermancour's attentions" (Brouard-Arends, 1991, 347).[7]

According to both literary and historical sources, however, the popularity of maternal themes in visual and textual productions of this period could be misleading. In their 1862 work *Women in the Eighteenth Century*, the Goncourt brothers wrote of the popularity of intimate genre painting in the late 1700s: "Let us take care however not to be fooled by these pretty family scenes, inspired not by the period's actual customs, but rather by its aspirations" (1982, 196).[8] In the late twentieth century, art historian Patricia Ivinski contended that "[t]he number of images of mothers breast-feeding [...] might lead viewers to the misconception that maternal nursing was the norm. On the contrary, the profusion of these works of art were meant to help fulfill the unrealized goal of making this myth a reality" (1998, 16). In *A Mother's Love*, Walker similarly cautioned her readers:

> Importantly, though, this idealized mother existed as a discursive dream at least a century before she became, in any substantive sense, reality. [...] The focus of my book is thus on the elaboration of a potent social fantasy; that is, the idealization of a wise and benevolent mother who may or may not have corresponded in any direct way with lived experience. (Walker, 2008, 25)

Like Walker, I will attempt to describe a series of representations of breast-feeding mothers which may or may not reflect the everyday realities of women from the eighteenth and nineteenth centuries.

So what was the reality of maternal breast-feeding in eighteenth-century France and how did it differ from the visual and literary representations? A brief overview of breast-feeding in the socio-historic context of the time will be useful in understanding the relationship between representation and reality.

Realities of Breast-Feeding in Eighteenth-Century France

Midwife Marie-Angélique Le Rebours, whose popular and practical 1767 handbook *Advice to Mothers Who Wish to Breast-Feed Their Children* was re-edited five times and translated into several languages by the end of the century, wrote in the first paragraph of her supplement to the third edition in 1775: "I observe with great satisfaction that the number of women who breast-feed their own children increases every day" (1775, iii). In the fifth edition, published in 1798, she indicated that she had omitted her previously published critique of *les gardes*, or baby nurses, stating that this critique had become obsolete not only because of the nurses' improved behavior, but also because "mothers are more able to judge them than they were in those days, when there were very few of them who breast-fed their own babies" (1798, 226).

Despite Le Rebours' optimism, however, ample evidence exists that the breast-feeding fad that peaked in the years immediately following the publication of Rousseau's *Emile* and *Julie* faded quickly, at least in Paris. The lieutenant-general of police in Paris, Jean LeNoir, compiled a statistical picture in 1780 indicating that, of the approximately 20,000 to 21,000 babies born in Paris that year, only about 700 were nursed by their mothers, or less than 5 percent (1780, 63). The medical community, whose members had been outspoken advocates for maternal nursing since the Renaissance, published innumerable treatises on the importance of maternal breast-feeding during the late eighteenth century in which they railed against French mothers for neglecting to nurse their children. In the preface to his 1772 work, *The Mother According to the Natural Order*, royal surgeon François Deleurye wrote that his book "has as its purpose to remind Mothers that nursing their own children is the most sacred of all duties" (1772, vi). Arguments cited in favor of maternal breast-feeding ranged from the health and welfare of both mother and child to the pernicious influence of ignorant, lower-class wet nurses. All these treatises acknowledged the pervasiveness of wet-nursing and the rate of infant mortality among babies sent out to nurse, which was estimated by Deleurye at 80 percent (xi).[9]

In 1779, the School of Medicine in Paris sponsored a competition that posed the following question: "What are the physical, moral and political advantages of mothers breast-feeding their children?" (Franklin, 1887–1902, vol. 19, p. 46).[10] A former student of the school, Doctor Landais, won first prize for his *Essay on the Advantages of the Breast-Feeding of Children by their Mothers*, published in 1781, in which he acknowledged that despite all the previous propaganda efforts, mothers continued to resist: "A thousand texts expound the usefulness and the endless advantages of maternal breast-feeding [...] There are truths that must be often repeated: to make them understood, to make them felt, one must say them for centuries, one must say them every day" (Landais, 1781, viii–viii).[11]

Nineteenth-century author George Sand tells us in her memoirs that her grandmother, Aurore Dupin de Francueil, insisted on nursing her son Maurice herself in Paris in 1778 due to her affection for the teachings of Rousseau:

> She wanted to nurse him herself, of course; that was still considered a bit eccentric, but she was one of those women who had read [Rousseau's] Emile religiously and who wanted to set a good example. Furthermore, she had an extremely well-developed maternal sentiment, and it was, for her, a passion that replaced all the others. But nature refused to answer her zeal. She had no milk, and for a few days, as she stubbornly continued to nurse her son despite horrendous suffering, she was able to feed him only with her blood. She had to give it up; for her, that was terribly painful and seemed to be a bad omen. (Sand, 1879, vol. 46, pp. 55–56)[12]

According to her granddaughter, the aristocratic Aurore Dupin de Francueil's stubborn insistence on nursing her own son was considered "eccentric" even in 1778, the supposed height of the breast-feeding fad that followed the publication of *Emile*.

Marie-Jeanne Roland, the famous intellectual and political figure of the revolutionary period and another fervent follower of Rousseau, wrote in a letter to her husband in November of 1781:

> Madame d'Eu gave birth to a little girl yesterday at noon . . . I went out this morning to go and visit them. [...] Good Lord! How bizarre a new mother looks when one finds her all alone,

with no child in sight! The poor baby was sucking her fingers and drinking cow's milk in a room far from her mother, waiting for the hired nurse who would breast-feed her. The father was in quite a hurry to have the baptism performed, in order to expedite the little creature's departure to the country. You know, my dear, I can't help myself – I think even less of them both after having witnessed their indifference. (Roland, 1900–2, 53)[13]

As social historian George Sussman has pointed out, Madame Roland's outrage is all the more poignant in that she was nursing her own six-week-old daughter at the time of the incident (1982, 80–81). Madame Roland wrote at length in her memoirs about her tireless efforts to breast-feed her daughter despite numerous obstacles, saying proudly: "I was a mother and a nurse (*nourrice*), while never ceasing to participate in my husband's work" (1864, 238).[14]

The following year, in 1782, Louis-Sébastien Mercier, in his chronicle of everyday Parisian life called *Tableau of Paris*, wrote:

Parisian mothers are no longer breast-feeding their children, and we dare say they're doing the right thing. It is not in the thick and fetid air of the capital, it is not in the midst of the tumult of business, it is not in the midst of the overly active or dissipated life of Paris that one can accomplish the duties of motherhood. Only in the country, by leading a balanced rustic life, can a woman nurse her own children without ruining her health. (Mercier, 1782–3, 145)[15]

This idyllic vision of country life versus city life typifies the beliefs of the period among well-to-do Parisians. Mercier goes on to praise the royal government for its increased vigilance in regulating the wet-nursing industry, calling the Parisian wet nurse bureau "a model of enlightened, active and vigilant management" (1782–3, 145).[16]

However, Mercier contradicts this support of the wet-nursing industry by implicitly criticizing parents' indifference in two other passages from the same work:

Saddled with yet another child, the bourgeois husband still goes drinking, while the newborn, handed over to a wet nurse, leaves for the country. The father and mother won't see him for two years, at which time the child, fleeing their embrace, will seek comfort in the bosom of the peasant woman whose milk he has drunk. [...] With wet nurses, governors, tutors, schools and convents, some women hardly notice that they are mothers. (1782–3, vols. 5–8, p. 57, vols. 1–4, p. 231)[17]

The scene of the child shrinking from his unfamiliar parents and clinging to his wet nurse, so vividly described by Mercier, can also be seen in numerous paintings and engravings of the period by Greuze, his follower Étienne Aubry, and others.[18] The subject remained popular through the early nineteenth century, as seen in Marguerite Gérard's painting from the Salon of 1804 (current location unknown) bearing this cumbersome title: "A Child Brought by his Wet-Nurse to his Mother, Whom He Refuses to Recognize" (Calley-Gallitz, 1998, 30 n. 28).[19] A contemporary Salon critic wrote of this painting: "Perhaps it will have strengthened the courage of some young wife ... May she follow the advice offered by this painting – how many tears will she be spared! It must be a cruel ordeal for a mother to see her child, even in the cradle, giving the lie to nature"(*Journal des arts*, 1805, 80–81).[20]

Mercier gives an idea of the prevalence of the wet-nursing industry in his critique of a study of population movements in France by Mr. Moheau, again in *Tableau of Paris* in 1782–3: "All the children who are born [in Paris] go out to a wet nurse, half of them die, and the registries of the parishes of Paris do not list their names; one can therefore rely neither on the registry of baptisms nor on the death registry for accurate figures" (Mercier, 1782–3, 322).[21] This casual account of an infant mortality rate of 50 percent among babies sent out to the country seems to run counter to Mercier's portrayal of an enlightened and vigilant administration of the wet-nursing industry. Most interesting for our purposes here, however, is his assertion that "*all* the children [...] go out to a wet nurse," emphasizing the universality of this custom in the capital in the 1780s.

Only a few years later, however, Mercier described a renaissance of maternal breast-feeding that stands in stark contrast to his earlier assessments in the *Tableau of Paris* of the 1780s. In *Paris during the Revolution, or The New Paris*, published in 1798, Mercier wrote an entire chapter on breast-feeding mothers ("*Les mères sont nourrices*"). In the year V of the Revolutionary calendar (1796), according to Mercier, wet nurses, a common sight in Paris prior to the Revolution, had disappeared from the streets and parks of the capital, and mothers nursing their children could be seen everywhere:

[W]hy not talk about a spectacle that at least brings consolation and that is constantly before our eyes? It is the spectacle offered by a multitude of children breast-fed by their mothers. [...] Never in any city, in any other time of my life, had I seen so many children. Motherhood is becoming for Frenchwomen an enhancement of their charms; they're all breast-feeding, they're all proud to be mothers and they all feel that the only good nurse is the true mother. Motherhood is so revered that its functions give the lie to all the idle gossip invented by malice and meanness. Their sex is justified for all its weaknesses as soon as it offers a caring and attentive nurse. (Mercier, 1862, 418)[22]

Similarly, Sussman quotes statistics from the year XI (1802–3) that seem to indicate a sharp increase in the number of infants nursed by their mothers in Paris during the Revolutionary period. According to a report to the General Council of Hospitals, of the 21,018 babies born in Paris that year, about half (10,667), were "nursed by their mothers," while the remaining half were either abandoned or sent out to a wet nurse (1982, 110). Sussman points out the unreliability of these statistics, however. According to him, the figure for children nursed by their mothers was derived simply from the total number of births minus the number of infants registered by the State wet-nursing bureau and the foundlings' bureau. He suggests the number of infants nursed by their mothers in year X only appeared to have increased since 1780 because the year X report did not take into account either children nursed in their own homes by live-in wet nurses (*nourrices sur lieu*) or those whose parents found wet nurses independently of the central bureau. Sussman also theorizes that there might have been a temporary decrease in live-in wet nurses in Paris during the revolutionary period due to social and economic upheaval and the difficulty of travel (1982, 110). The accuracy of these statistics remains in question, then, particularly in light of Sussman's observations on the diminishing influence and prestige of the official wet-nursing bureau after the Revolution and the rise of free enterprise in the placement of nurslings outside Paris throughout the nineteenth century.

If there was in fact a surge in maternal breast-feeding in the final decade of the eighteenth century, it seems to have been brief. In 1825, well after the revolutionary period and during the Restoration of the monarchy, Father Besnard published a moralistic treatise written in

1779 for the School of Medicine's *concours*, in which it had won an honorable mention. His work bore the descriptive, if heavy-handed, title: *Perils to Which Are Exposed Children Whose Mothers Refuse to Breast-Feed Them, and Misfortunes These Mothers Bring upon Themselves by This Refusal.* In his 1825 updates to the 1779 text, Besnard decried the short-lived nature of the breast-feeding fad:

> The immortal pages written by Rousseau on this subject inspired such enthusiasm that most mothers of his day, in emulation of each other, chose to breast-feed their own children. The custom soon became nearly universal, *even among the upper classes.* But in France, everything is usually ephemeral [...] It is thus no longer fashionable today for mothers to give their children the only food suited to them. (Besnard, 1825, 6–8; my emphasis)[23]

The unsigned preface to Besnard's work (dated 1825, and possibly written by Madame Huzard, his editor), confirms these observations: "Following the writings of J.-J. Rousseau on this subject, all mothers, at one time, breast-fed their children; it was the fashion. Soon, however, the difficulties and the various burdens of the household and of life brought this fashion to an end, and the writer who introduced it was more or less dismissed as a dreamer" (1825, i).

Why did the breast-feeding campaign that had seen such success in the 1760s and 1770s, and perhaps again (briefly) during the revolutionary period, fade so quickly? Social historians such as Catherine Rollet and George Sussman have proposed many possible explanations, ranging from socio-economic factors to cultural tendencies. Mothers of the poorest classes had never stopped breast-feeding, simply because they could not afford even the cheapest wet nurse; they did, however, take advantage of the option of abandoning their children. Mercier estimates that between 7,000 and 8,000 children were left at the orphanage each year in Paris, most because their parents could not afford to keep them. These children were sent out to wet nurses in the country, where, according to Mercier, about two-thirds died before the age of five (1782–83, 235). Wives of city merchants and artisans, on the other hand, depended on various forms of childcare, including wet-nursing, to free them for the everyday duties of helping their husbands in the shop or workshop. Most of this group could not afford the option of breast-feeding with its unavoidable effects on their daily work lives, whatever Rousseau may have told them.

What of the more privileged classes? If we are to believe Madame Huzard, many of them shunned breast-feeding because it interfered with the duties of running a household and the other activities of a well-to-do woman of the period. Despite Rousseau's and others' attempts to convince these ladies that the call of nature could not and should not be ignored, they continued to see breast-feeding as vulgar, animalistic, and somewhat disgusting. In the pseudo-memoirs of aristocrat Madame d'Epinay, written between 1770 and 1780, the heroine writes a letter to her husband requesting his permission to breast-feed their child, and his response illustrates the upper-class reaction to such a concept: "You, breast-feed your child? I thought I would die laughing. Even if you were strong enough, do you really think I would agree to such a ridiculous notion?" (1951, vol. 1, p. 295).[24] The term "ridiculous" should be taken in the strongest sense here; the husband is concerned about what others of their social milieu would think of his wife (and, by extension, himself) were she to breast-feed. The husband continues: "My dear one, whatever the opinions of obstetricians and doctors may be, put that notion right out of your head. It lacks common sense. What the hell kind of satisfaction can one find in nursing a child?" (vol. 1, p. 295).[25]

This dismissive attitude of the privileged classes was reinforced by Madame de Genlis's best-selling treatise on women's education, *Adele and Theodore*, published in 1782. Written in part as a response to Rousseau's *Émile*, Genlis's epistolary work offers an alternative version of women's education that seemed quite different from that of Rousseau in several respects, not the least of which was the lack of importance of breast-feeding. In *Adele and Theodore*, the baroness writes to her grown daughter who is considering nursing her child: "Nature has no doubt imposed upon us the sweet obligation to breast-feed our children, and we may only be excused from that obligation when we are forced by other duties that are even more essential" (1801, 166).[26] The wife's duty to her husband and to his social advancement counts among those duties, and while the baroness stops short of telling her daughter not to breast-feed, her advice is to do so only "if, without doing harm to his interests or his fortune, you can close yourself up in the interior of your family for a year, eighteen months, and perhaps two years" (167). She then tells a story of a society lady who would parade her baby in front of company. "The mother would let her baby nurse, in front of seven or eight men; I saw these men laughing amongst themselves and whispering to each other, and all this seemed merely indecent and importunate to me" (167). Public ridicule again appears as a strong argument against breast-feeding. In order to be successful at breast-feeding, the baroness contends that a lady would have to give up appearing in society altogether and focus all her energies on her child, which would create a serious social handicap for herself and for her husband. As Annie Smart has noted:

> Genlis suggests that nature should never disrupt the social order. While breast-feeding is a "douce obligation," women must bend their will to the duties imposed by their social rank ("d'autres devoirs plus essentiels encore"). New mothers should thus be willing to sacrifice their personal wish to nurse their child if the interests of their husband's family require them to do so. Breast-feeding for the sake of the child seems almost selfish, in Genlis's terms: a woman should think first of her husband and his station in society; and, if he opposes, she must submit to his authority, even if it means forsaking nursing her own child. (Smart, 2011, 89)

Unlike Rousseau's contention that public morality could be restored by mothers nursing their own children, Genlis clearly stated that social imperatives made this laudable goal impractical and nearly impossible for aristocratic women.

In addition, certain wealthy women in France by the end of the eighteenth century had managed to rise to a level of social importance and political involvement that they were loath to relinquish. This social status resulted in part from the *précieuse* movement in the previous century as well as from the eighteenth-century *salons* led by well-educated, well-spoken, and well-read ladies, *salons* in which these women dictated the way well-bred men should act, talk, dress, and even write. As can be seen in the works of Molière and others, the *précieuses* sought to focus on things of the mind and deny their bodies, inventing bizarre euphemisms for bodily functions and requiring suitors to adore them platonically, not physically. Childbirth and breast-feeding served as stark and often unwelcome reminders of their own physicality. In addition, the everyday tasks of nursing and caring for an infant might present certain challenges to parents running a social *salon* or writing poetry. Indeed, both Montaigne and Rousseau admitted that they could not think and write with children running about. Montaigne sent his six daughters out to a wet nurse, where, he writes with careless imprecision, "two or three" of them died; only one of them, Leonora, survived to adulthood (Montaigne, 1595, vol. 1, p. 158). Rousseau abandoned all five of his children by his mistress Thérèse at the foundlings' home. He later claimed in his *Confessions* that, not only had he acted to preserve his mistress's honor, but he also believed it to be in the children's best interest to be raised by the State, due to his inability to provide for them (Book 9, vol. 2, p. 139).

In an article on redefining motherhood during the Enlightenment, Valerie Lastinger analyzed the gradual separation of sexuality and maternity in the new definition of womanhood during the eighteenth century. While the writers of the *Encyclopédie* still wavered between the aesthetic and maternal function of the breast, she argued, by the 1770s physicians and philosophers agreed that the sole purpose of woman was to produce and nurse babies, which would keep women safely in the private sphere and away from politics. According to Lastinger, "[a]lthough on the surface the revival of maternal nursing had infant survival as its main purpose, one prime consequence was to tie women to the home more securely at a time when women in France were becoming a strong political force. Maternal nursing was Nature's answer to the growing concern among the French intellectual and religious establishment about a steady population decline and a growing involvement of women in public life" (1996, 603). By keeping mothers in the home, Frenchmen could both ensure the survival of the French nation and limit the political involvement of women that was a cause of great anxiety before and during the Revolution. It is hardly surprising that women of the time, particularly upper-class women, resisted this pressure to abandon their *salons* and withdraw into the private sphere of the family. We will see in the next chapter how Napoleon reinforced this concept of maternal and domestic duty, both in his own beliefs and in the far-reaching legal document known as the Napoleonic Code.

Other possible cultural explanations of the reluctance to breast-feed include the widely held belief, at once medical, popular, and theological, that sexual intercourse during lactation would spoil a woman's milk. While some doctors were beginning to refute this theory (Puzos, 1759, 231), it remained a part of both cultural practice and Catholic doctrine for most of the eighteenth and nineteenth centuries. The article on childhood illnesses in Diderot's *Encyclopédie* cites "wet nurses' overindulgence in sexual intercourse" as a prime cause of illness among nurslings (*Encyclopédie*, 1751–72, vol. 5, p. 67).[27] Doctor Roze de l'Epinoy, writing in 1785, recommended not only that the nursing woman abstain from coitus during breast-feeding, but that she bear this privation cheerfully ("sans chagrin"), at the risk of spoiling her milk (1785, 9).

As for Catholic doctrine, the Church's teachings on breast-feeding were often contradictory and seemed to place the blame on women both for nursing and for refusing to do so. The *Encyclopédie* article on the wet nurse or the breast-feeding woman (*la nourrice*), published in 1765, stated that "the Church fathers" considered any mother who refused to breast-feed, "a barbarous unnatural mother" (vol. 11, p. 260).[28] On the other hand, in the *Abridged Dictionary of Questions of Conscience*, published just one year earlier (Pontas, 1764), good Catholics learned that if the husband "is at risk of incontinence, the wife must, if she can, give her child to a wet nurse so she can tend to her husband's infirmity"[29] This implied that if the husband sinned, either by adultery or by masturbation, the wife would be held responsible before God. Historian Jean-Louis Flandrin has theorized that nursing mothers might have been discouraged from fulfilling their conjugal duty by the Church due to the potential corruption of their milk should they become pregnant. According to Flandrin, "[b]ecause they accepted neither contraception nor conjugal infidelity, Catholic theologians had found in wet-nursing the solution to the incompatibility of the roles of mother and wife" (1976, 222).[30] For the wife who wished to keep her husband faithful, and thus virtuous, as well as avoid any risk to the child, wet-nursing remained the only viable option.[31]

By the 1780s, then, for a wide variety of reasons, most infants born in Paris to aristocratic and bourgeois families, as well as a large proportion of those born into poorer circumstances, were being raised by provincial wet nurses, hired either by the families or by the foundlings' bureau. Cultural, social, and economic pressures caused an unprecedented boom in the wet-nursing industry, which previously served primarily the very rich and the very poor.

Breast-Feeding Manuals in Eighteenth-Century France

> One must take great care with the nursing woman's lifestyle: what she eats, what she drinks, her sleeping and waking habits, exercise and rest, and regulate them according to the disposition and needs of the child; she will avoid all foods that heat up the blood, such as spices, pastries, salty foods, mustard, strong unwatered wines, and especially anger, and all things that burn the blood. (Paré, 1573, 118–19)[32]

As we can see from this excerpt of French barber-surgeon Ambroise Paré's 1573 treatise, *Of the Reproduction of Man, and the Way of Extracting Infants from the Mother's Womb,* breast-feeding instruction manuals such as the twentieth-century La Leche League's *Womanly Art of Breast-Feeding* are far from a recent phenomenon. In France as well as elsewhere in Europe, published texts addressed the subjects of childbirth and nursing as early as the sixteenth century. Paré, royal surgeon to Henri II and his sons, devoted no fewer than nine chapters to the selection, care, and feeding of the breast-feeding woman. Written in French, likely because Paré as a barber-surgeon lacked the formal medical training that would have made him fluent in Latin, this treatise was therefore accessible to the literate French public. For the women who attended the midwifery school founded by Paré in Paris, his treatise must have been not only accessible, but extremely useful. Having become famous for an earlier work on treating gunshot wounds on the battlefield, Paré based his recommendations largely on his own practical observation. Reprinted dozens of times in the sixteenth and seventeenth centuries, translated into Latin, English, and numerous other languages, Paré's works became a standard reference on pediatric medicine throughout the Western world.

While other breast-feeding texts written in French by doctors or moralists such as Laurent Joubert (1578) and Philippe Hecquet (1704) appeared sporadically from the late sixteenth to the mid-eighteenth centuries, the years following the publication of Rousseau's *Émile* saw a veritable explosion of publications on the subject. At least twenty how-to (or how-*not*-to) manuals appeared in France between 1762 and 1800, with colorful and interminable titles such as Pierre-François Nicolas's *The Call of Nature, On Behalf of Newborns; Volume in Which the Pregnant and Nursing Woman's Diet is Outlined, as Well as the Advantages and Joys of Nursing one's Own Children; and the Dangers Women Run, by Refusing to Submit to this Law of Nature* (Nicolas, 1775). Why were so many such texts published during this period? Why did mothers of the Enlightenment (albeit only the ones wealthy and educated enough to acquire and read books) suddenly need, and were suddenly willing to buy, all this advice?

Dr. Gaultier de Claubry, Surgeon of His Royal Highness the Count d'Artois, Member of the Royal College of Surgery, and Birth Attendant; former Surgeon Major of the King's Army in Germany (this according to the modest title page of his 1783 tome, *New Advice for Women Who Wish to Breast-Feed*), claimed that the need for instructional tracts on breast-feeding stemmed from the abyss between contemporary mothers and the ways of nature, or "the primitive state" (1783, 4). In addition, argued the good doctor, "young women whose mothers did not nurse, deprived of domestic advice and role models, are ignorant of a thousand little things that, in the details, seem to be of little import, but which as a whole contribute to the success of breast-feeding" (4–5).[33] (Interestingly, the La Leche League, founded in the USA in 1956, used this same argument to explain its usefulness to twentieth-century mothers whose own mothers had bottle-fed them.)

Logically, however, Gaultier de Claubry's argument only holds if Frenchwomen of this period *were* in fact more likely to nurse their own children than their mothers had been. On this point, as we have seen, the historical evidence is scarce and often contradictory. In the second edition of her *Advice to Mothers Who Wish to Nurse*, published in 1770, midwife Madame Le Rebours wrote, in reference to another breast-feeding treatise published in 1750, "[T]he lack of progress made by natural feeding since that time proves […] that one does not always benefit as much as one should from the efforts of enlightened and humane people to share with others the fruits of their meditations and experience" (1770, 68).[34] However, as we saw earlier, according to the preface of the third edition in 1775, the situation had changed.[35]

We have seen the contradictory evidence on the number of breast-feeding mothers throughout the final decades of the eighteenth century, including the writings of Sebastien Mercier and Abbot Besnard among others. Whether the number of nursing mothers actually increased in the last quarter of the eighteenth century or not, many authors evidently believed that the reading public would benefit from the publication of "a few useful works," in the words of Gaultier de

Claubry, most of which were written by officially sanctioned medical authorities like himself.

A survey of the treatises of the period, however, produces an impression that their main purpose was not to instruct women on the practical details of successful breast-feeding, but rather to persuade reluctant French mothers to breast feed in the first place. In the preface to his 1772 work, *The Mother According to the Natural Order,* royal surgeon François Deleurye wrote that his book "has as its purpose to remind Mothers that nursing their own Children is the most sacred of all duties" (1772, vi).[36] Arguments cited in favor of maternal breast-feeding ranged from the health and welfare of both mother and child to the pernicious influence of ignorant, lower-class wet nurses. All these treatises acknowledged the pervasiveness of wet-nursing and the rate of infant mortality among babies sent out to nurse.

One short pamphlet entitled *Advice to Mothers Who Intend to Nurse Their Own Children, on a Way to Help Them in This Difficult Occupation,* written by a surgeon named Bru in 1780, provided the recipe for a gruel that he claimed was safe to use as a supplement if a frail upper-class woman did not have sufficient milk for her baby, as had supposedly happened to the author's wife. Bru proposed this supplemental feeding technique as a safer alternative than using a wet nurse, since the parents could maintain control over the infant's care (1780, 7). Most of these treatises also include lengthy sections on the circumstances that might prevent mothers from breast-feeding as well as detailed instructions on choosing a good wet nurse. In fact, the author of a 1785 book deceptively entitled *Advice to Mothers Who Want to Nurse* waited until the last lines of his preface to reveal that "the sole purpose that I propose here is to determine which mothers should not breast-feed" (Roze de l'Epinoy, 1785, vii).[37]

In this atmosphere of breast-feeding propaganda, one treatise of the period stands out as a source of practical and detailed instruction for the breast-feeding mother: *Advice to Mothers Who Want to Nurse their Children* by midwife Marie Angélique Le Rebours. Cited by Madame Roland as a fount of practical knowledge on breast-feeding, "whose wisdom and exactitude I cannot praise enough" (Sussman, 1982, 81), Madame Le Rebours' handy pocket-sized manual, first published in 1767, had been reprinted at least six times by the end of the century. Le Rebours wrote in a letter to Rousseau (which accompanied a first edition of her work for his perusal) that she had wanted to nurse her daughter who was born before the publication of *Émile* but had been prevented from doing so. In her next pregnancy, her determination reinforced by her reading of *Émile*, she resolved:

> to brave all opposition [...] The fear of worrying my husband about my health, or of quarreling with my parents, or of neglecting my talent for painting, the example of several women I knew who, instead of succeeding at nursing, had had to give it up after much suffering, the aggravation of having three small children in the house and very little help, all these difficulties did not stop me. (Rousseau, 1979, 216)[38]

In the preface, Le Rebours states that she purposely placed the practical advice in the first chapter of her book, saving the arguments in favor of maternal breast-feeding for a later chapter, because "my first and main purpose has been to spare women who intend to breast-feed the pain and the difficulties that many of them might suffer for lack of knowing what they are supposed to do" (1770, xxvi).[39]

Immediately following the preface to the second edition (1770), the reader will find a letter of recommendation from the influential Swiss doctor Samuel Tissot, author of the best-selling 1761 treatise *Advice to the People on Their Health* and an established medical authority of the Enlightenment. Dr. Tissot praised Le Rebours in the following terms:

> I know of no other work that could do so much good; and its potential for good is even greater because, since it is the work of a respectable woman, who tells only what she has done and seen, people will have more confidence in this work than in those of Doctors. (Le Rebours, 1770, xxx–xxxi)[40]

Presumably the "people" to whom Tissot refers are new mothers, intended readers of the manual, who would be more likely to trust the advice of a woman and mother like themselves. Abbot Besnard recommended Le Rebours' book to his sister-in-law in his own treatise, saying it was

> made by a lady who had a great number of children that she raised herself, none of whom died; and who, by her industry, her reflections, and her long experience, has managed to make the art of raising children accessible to all mothers, whatever their

condition, their situation, or their profession, by rendering its practice singularly simple. (Besnard, 1825, 79)[41]

The second edition of *Advice to Mothers* in 1770 also included an endorsement from a committee of the School of Medicine in Paris, stating "that it is to be hoped that this Work will reach more and more of the public, and that all mothers will adhere to it in every detail" (Le Rebours, 1770, xxxiv).[42]

Although the author cited recommendations by male doctors as proof of the value of her book, she never claimed to base her advice on scientific knowledge: "I have not the science of Doctors, but I have practical experience" (xiii).[43] Indeed, the first chapter contains a treasure trove of practical tips for nursing mothers on important questions such as when to nurse the baby for the first time (at birth), how to avoid sore nipples (through proper positioning), how to treat plugged ducts (with compresses of milk and bread) and even how to extract milk from a painfully engorged breast (by heating the bottom of a small apothecary's bottle and applying the opening to the breast). While other authors wrote hundreds of pages explaining why women should breast-feed their children or illustrating the dire consequences that would befall them if they did not, Le Rebours offered something much more useful, particularly for a nervous new mother lacking the domestic support network described by Gaultier de Claubry: in short, a realistic instruction manual with guaranteed results. "I say only things of which I am sure. If you follow my advice exactly, you will be certain of success" (1770, 22–23).[44]

Judging from the published reactions of her contemporaries, Le Rebours seemed to have succeeded in her quest to enlighten the public on breast-feeding techniques. Gaultier de Claubry cited Le Rebours' book among the "few useful works" mentioned earlier in this study, the only one on his list to be written by a woman (1783, 5–6). Madame Roland, in *Advice to my Daughter at the Age and in the Situation of Becoming a Mother*, written in prison in 1793, recommended Le Rebours' volume to her daughter in the strongest possible terms (1798–99, vol. 1, pp. 305–6). Most impressive, however, is the emphasis placed on Le Rebours' work by the most prestigious and all-encompassing fount of knowledge of the period: Diderot and d'Alembert's *Encyclopédie*. Although the article "breast-feeding" ("*allaitement*") in the original edition of the *Encyclopédie*, published a decade or so before Madame

Le Rebours' text, consisted of only a few lines, the 1776 supplement included an eleven-page article on the same subject. The article begins with a scholarly explanation of the physical origins of milk and the nefarious effects of its suppression on the mother's body. After having established the desirability of maternal breast-feeding, the author writes:

> Now I need only explain what one must do to succeed in breast-feeding. I believe I could find no better guide in this than Madame Le Rebours, whose experience, well-exercised judgement and knowledge beyond the norm for her sex have enabled her to instruct women wishing to acquit themselves of their maternal duties. (Diderot, 1776, vol. 1, p. 293)[45]

The author then proceeds, in the remaining four pages, to summarize the first chapter of Le Rebours' book, illustrating the influence and widespread reputation of her work in France in the final decades of the eighteenth century.

Even as late as 1804, Parisian doctor Jean Verdier-Heurtin mentioned Le Rebours in his medical thesis on nursing, calling her one of the "most enlightened partisans of maternal breast-feeding" (1804, 20).[46] Despite this passing mention, however, the fame of Madame Le Rebours as well as the popularity of treatises like hers seem to wane with the turn of the century. From 1798, the date of the last edition of her book, until the mid-nineteenth century, practical breast-feeding manuals were few and far between, although dozens of male medical students in France during this same period earned their degrees with theses on the sacred duty of maternal breast-feeding that merely repeated the same old arguments. One possible explanation for this dearth of practical knowledge in print could be the gradual domination of the field of childbirth and child-rearing by male practitioners throughout the nineteenth century. Writing in 1842, Dr. Alfred Donné ("medical doctor, former director of the clinic of the School of Medicine in Paris, professor of microscopy, etc.") condemned the mothering manuals of the late eighteenth century for their lack of scientific grounding:

> A few of these volumes were not entirely useless at the time they were published, in combating customs that were obviously contrary to the well-being and the best interest of children; but

none of them establishes rules according to observation of facts and scientific methods. (Donné, 1842, vi)[47]

Since women were forbidden during this period from attending the institutions that provided formal scientific training, this emphasis on "scientific methods" would have meant the exclusion of Le Rebours' work from the accepted body of medical knowledge on pediatrics. As Sonia Boon has noted, "located within a system of non-institutionalised knowledge transmission Madame Le Rebours, as a midwife, also operated from a perspective that appeared to bypass the authority of 'medical science' in favour of a gynocentric practice that emphasised the power of maternal sharing and community" (Boon, 2009, 10).

Forty years later came another example of the co-opting of breast-feeding by the male establishment: Cora Millet-Robinet, scientist, author, and mother of five, whose similarly popular practical breast-feeding manual, *Advice to Young Women on their Condition and their Maternal Duties while Breast-Feeding*, of 1841, went through several editions throughout the nineteenth century. Valerie Lastinger's analysis of Millet-Robinet's work characterized her as a scientist, raised in a scientific family alongside her brother, who became a chemist, and trained, albeit informally, in scientific methods of observation (2012, 175–89). Despite this informal scientific background, Millet-Robinet apparently based her writings on her own life experience, much as Le Rebours purportedly had done. Millet-Robinet opened her work with the line: "Having observed a lot, reflected often, and having thus acquired a certain level of experience, I may have a few useful ideas" (178). As the century progressed, a woman's practical observations, however scientific, were no longer adequate for the educated reader. In 1884, Millet-Robinet collaborated with Dr. Émile Allix ("Doctor and inspector of the service of child protection and of childcare facilities in Paris," according to the title page) in producing a new and very different version of her work. In the introduction to the new edition, the editor explained that, despite the obvious success of Millet-Robinet's previous books, there had always been something missing:

[I]n a work intended to serve as a guide to young mothers, there is an entire series of special issues that cannot be completely addressed without the collaboration of a doctor. (Millet-Robinet and Allix, 1897, v)[48]

The "practical experience" of Le Rebours and Millet-Robinet, no longer valued by the medical establishment, was displaced by a growing number of medical texts that in many instances directly contradicted the common-sense advice of Le Rebours. These texts advocated such practices as feeding the infant on a strict schedule (Donné, 1842, 115)[49] and weighing the infant every day to ensure proper weight gain (Toussaint, 1887, 91).[50]

It would take mothering manuals another hundred years, until the late twentieth century, to debunk these supposedly scientifically determined practices and rediscover the "practical experience" of breast-feeding mothers. On the website of La Leche League France, we learn that since its founding in 1956 the League "has never ceased challenging the dictates of health professionals with the lived experience of mothers: the importance of early breast-feeding, feeding on demand, without schedules or intervals, night feedings […] the respect for children's needs (looking at the baby rather than the clock or the scale) […] exactly the opposite of everything that professionals and manuals of the period recommended" (Didierjean-Jouveau, 2003).[51] On the back cover of the seventh edition of La Leche League's bestselling book, *The Womanly Art of Breast-Feeding*, published in 2004, the editors claim that in 1963, the date of the first edition, it was "the first book of its kind, written for mothers by mothers." Marie-Angélique Le Rebours' immensely popular pocket-sized manual, published two centuries earlier, proves them wrong. Midwife, mother, and author, Le Rebours was a female pioneer in breast-feeding advocacy; although her book was later discredited by the male medical establishment, much of its practical advice remains as relevant today as so many women obviously found it to be in late eighteenth-century France.

Political Discourse on Breast-Feeding during the Revolutionary Period

The revolutionary fascination with breast-feeding as a political symbol has been described at length by Mary Jacobus (1995) and Marilyn Yalom (1997). As Yalom points out: "Nursing was no longer a private matter with ramifications only for the infant and its family. It had become, as Rousseau had hopefully envisioned, a collective manifestation of civic duty" (1997, 117). Ruth Perry described the new cultural discourse constructing women's bodies "as maternal rather than sexual" (1991, 213). At the Festival of Regeneration, a revolutionary fête held in August 1793 in Paris, the president of the Convention, Hérault de Séchelles, stood before a larger-than-life statue of Nature with water shooting from her breasts. The inscription on the fountain read: "We are all her children" (Jacobus, 1995, 222). As he filled his cup, Hérault de Séchelles proclaimed: "May these fertile waters that flow from your breasts [...] consecrate in this cup of fraternity and equality the vows that France makes to you this day!" Later the same day, beneath a triumphal arch, he waxed even more eloquent in his praises of republican motherhood: "May all soldierly and generous virtues flow, with maternal milk, into the hearts of all the nurslings of France!" (1793, 3–5).[52] Maternal milk thus became an integral part of the symbolism of the nascent French republic and the virtues that the new order sought to encourage in its citizens. Jacobus interpreted the representations of this event, in which only men drank from the fountain, as "the visually dominant, ideologically charged, abstract image of the State as Mother Republic" (1995, 222). This maternal Republic, nurturing and nourishing her children–citizens, replaced the iconography of the monarch as father of the people, particularly after the beheading of Louis XVI earlier that year.

Another example of the political rhetoric surrounding the act of breast-feeding can be seen in the passionate speech of Citizen Dulaurent on November 10, 1793, on the occasion of the Festival of Reason. In a clear allusion to the law of June 28 of that year, which made maternal breast-feeding mandatory for all mothers receiving State support, Dulaurent exclaimed:

> Oh! Why, when motherhood offers such pleasures, are there beings *so unnatural* as to forget its primary duties and fail to recognize its charms? How is it that mothers have been seen to command that the innocent creature to which they just gave birth be whisked from their sight! Fortunately, such monsters are rare on this earth! Fortunately, the law is there to avenge Nature! (Dulaurent, 1793, 13)[53]

However, as Dulaurent continued his harangue, it became evident that such "monsters" were more common than he would like us to believe. After calling down all sorts of eloquent curses on these unnatural mothers, he expressed the following wish for all the mothers who might be listening: "[M]ay the day soon come when you will be able freely to tear away the veil you have thrown over nature" (1793, 18–19).[54] This implies that many mothers had strayed from the precepts of Nature as defined by the Rousseauist revolutionary government and were not in fact breast-feeding their own children in 1793.

Most State attempts to encourage, or even to force, mothers to breast-feed their children in the late eighteenth century went hand in hand with the concept of public assistance born during the Revolution. The Constitution of 1791 proclaimed: "A general institution of Public Assistance shall be created and organized to raise abandoned children, care for the infirm poor, and offer work to the physically able poor who could not find work otherwise" (*Constitution de 1791*).[55] Social historian Rachel Fuchs pointed out that "officials of the First Republic believed that it was one's duty to have children in order to perpetuate the spirit of liberty and that the welfare of children should receive the highest priority" (1992, 100). Louis de Saint-Just, a writer and ideologue who participated in the French Revolution and was a member of the Convention before his execution in 1794, wrote in his treatise on Republican institutions: "The mother who has not nursed her baby ceases to be a mother in the eyes of the fatherland" (Blum, 1986, 190). In June 1793, the National Convention issued a decree attaching one important condition to public assistance of newborns: "Those who apply for assistance that is due to them in the name of their unborn child will be obligated to agree that the child will be nursed by its mother" (*Décret relatif à l'organisation des secours à accorder annuellement aux enfants*, 1793, titre 1, art. 26).[56] Most radically of all, unlike most private charitable organizations such as the Society of Maternal Charity, founded in 1784, the Convention specifically extended the right to public assistance to unwed mothers, but again only if they agreed to nurse their own infants (*Décret*, 1793, titre 2, art. 4).[57] Unfortunately, however, the short-lived First Republic had limited resources and its ambitious plans for public assistance remained mostly unenforced and unrealized.

Yalom tells the story of citizen Elisabeth Le Bas, whose husband Philippe Le Bas was executed during the coup against Robespierre in 1794. His last words to his wife, mother of their newborn son, seemed to equate breast-feeding with patriotism: "Nourish him with your own milk [...] Inspire in him the love of his country" (1997, 114). Yalom interprets this obsession with maternal breast-feeding as symbolic of Republican values:

In the revolutionary discourse, the pure milk of loving mothers was implicitly compared with the tainted milk of *ancien régime* aristocrats, most of whom were raised by wet nurses. This pairing of maternal nursing with republican virtues and wet nurses with royalist decadence allowed women a "patriotic" choice: those who chose to suckle their young could be seen as making a political statement in favor of the new regime. (Yalom, 1997, 116)

I would add that the pressure on new mothers to breast-feed served multiple purposes in this period. Its political significance as a symbol of Republican patriotic duty doubled as a convenient means, as we have seen, of keeping women confined in the private sphere and out of politics. While the symbolic female figure of Marianne, the avatar of the French Republic, granted new mythic status to the concept of the feminine as leader and mother of the new nation, actual Frenchwomen were actively discouraged from participating in revolutionary policy-making.

As Madelyn Gutwirth has noted in her study of visual representations of women during the Revolution, "The other side of this tidal wave of insistence on maternal nursing is that it never really worked, at least in Paris" (1992, 183). Despite enormous cultural and political pressure in the final decades of the eighteenth century, French women who could afford it continued for the most part to resist this "mode de la mamelle (fashion for the teat)," as Gutwirth puts it, hiring wet nurses instead to feed their babies (183). Poor Parisian women who had to find childcare so they could make a living continued to hire even poorer wet nurses out in the country. Gutwirth concluded that despite a brief decline in the number of infants sent out to wet nurses during the Revolutionary period, "[t]he practice of wet-nursing, as a response to material necessity, was not eradicated by a war of ideas" (183).

Literary and visual representations of mothers breast-feeding their children, so frequent during the final decades of the eighteenth century, would see a rapid decline in the first decades of the nineteenth with the rise of Romanticism and the reign of Napoleon, who firmly believed that women belonged in the home. In the next chapter, we will examine a few of the reasons for this decrease in representation after the turn of the century.

Chapter 2

The Absence of the Breast
in the Tale of the Romantic Hero

In his book entitled *Sick Heroes: French Society and Literature in the Romantic Age, 1750–1850*, Allan Pasco theorized that the virtual absence of the mother from the tale of the Romantic hero originated with the custom of placing babies with a wet nurse from birth (1997). According to Pasco, entire generations of French authors would grow up with no affective attachments to their parents, which would in turn create the cultural phenomenon of the melancholic Romantic hero that dominated French literature in the early decades of the nineteenth century. But are there other, less obvious explanations for the paucity of representations of nursing mothers during this period?

One possible explanation stems from the increasingly repressive laws set down in the legal document known as the Napoleonic Code, which relegated even the most wealthy, privileged women to the private sphere. These laws, made up of a combination of existing common law and Napoleon's concept of a public sphere dominated by men, codified the misogynist reactions to the active participation of women in the Revolution, placing women and mothers firmly under the legal tutelage of their husbands.

Another explanation can be gleaned from a textual analysis of the Romantic works that depict breast-feeding. When the nursing mother does appear, she is often depicted as a marginalized figure, either by cultural or racial background or by non-normative behaviors such as delusions or excessive grieving. Chateaubriand exhibits a morbid fascination with native American women, who demonstrated their maternal devotion by sprinkling their milk over the graves of their dead infants. For him, these scenes serve as an illustration of the native people's closeness to nature: "Shall we tell of the tenderness of the mother bear who, like the female savage, takes maternal love to the extreme by nursing her young after their death?" (1803, 210).[1] This valorization of natural motherhood, reminiscent of Rousseau's descriptions of the "good savage," focuses on indigenous people, whereas in Chateaubriand's works, the French mother breast-feeding her child is largely absent.

Similarly, Victor Hugo portrays the grieving mother of a nursling in two poems: "Fiat voluntas" (1837) (Hugo, 1964, 1053–54) and "The Ghost" (1842) (Hugo, 1922, 245). Rather than glorifying motherhood for its benefits to both mother and child as well as to the nation, as we saw in the previous century, these Romantic authors showed us the dark side of maternal devotion, the ways in which mothers react to loss and grief. Even when they created positive representations of nursing mothers, as with Lamartine's autobiographical writings about his mother, these maternal figures retained overtones of tragedy and loss, setting the scene for the Romantic hero to set out on a journey of self-discovery; as Lesley Walker puts it, "a search for lost love – which will eventually make him an ethical man and citizen" (2008, 28).

In this chapter, I will explore the various reasons for the scarcity of textual and visual representations of breast-feeding mothers in France in the early decades of the nineteenth century.

Napoleon and the Disappearing Mother

For an entire generation of Frenchmen growing up during the revolutionary period, Napoleon Bonaparte embodied the post-revolutionary dream of social ascension in a time of shifting socio-political norms. The account of his rise to power in the *Mémorial de Sainte-Hélène* inspired Romantic heroes such as Julien Sorel in Stendhal's *Le Rouge et le noir*. His influence, formalized in the Napoleonic Code, would dominate aspects of French culture for more than a century, including cultural norms and laws regarding women in general and mothers in particular.

According to June Burton, in *Napoleon and the Woman Question*, Dr. Pierre Jean Georges Cabanis, a disciple of Roussel and protégé of Napoleon, used the emerging science of psychophysiology and its glandular secretion theories to prove that women were biologically unfit for public life. According to Cabanis, women, in order to remain healthy, needed to engage in such normal female behaviors as gestation and lactation and to avoid activities such as philosophy or literature for which they were ill suited (2007, 139). Cabanis's theories must have seemed convenient to Napoleon, since they meshed with his views on women's limited role in society.

Numerous anecdotes illustrate Napoleon's ideas about women. Madame Campan recalled the time when Napoleon interrupted Germaine de Staël during a heated political argument to ask whether she had nursed her children (1824, 82). On another occasion, when Staël asked him to name the woman in history whom he most admired, he infamously replied: "The one who had the most children" (Knibiehler and Fouquet, 1980, 168).[2] There is little doubt that Napoleon cared very much about controlling women's bodies, but historians Yvonne Knibiehler and Catherine Fouquet go one step further, stating that Napoleon saw the female body primarily as a "baby machine," or "the mold of brave men" (168).[3] Napoleon is said to have asked a woman who had given birth to twenty-four children, "When is the twenty-fifth?" to which she responded graciously, "I am at Your Majesty's disposal" (169).[4] Finally, after the battle of Eylau, in which estimates of French casualties range from 18,000 to 22,000 men, Napoleon was reported to have remarked, "Bah! One night in Paris will make up for all of that" (169).[5] According to Knibiehler and Fouquet, "This realistic objective eliminates all idealization, all exaltation of maternity. On this point, Napoleon regresses to before Rousseau and the Convention" (168–69).[6]

His view of women as baby machines had a few positive effects in terms of public policy. When the Empress Marie Louise became pregnant in 1810, Napoleon expressed an increased interest in the welfare of pregnant mothers and especially that of their offspring (Adams, 2010, 58). In a decree dated July 28, 1811, Napoleon reorganized the Society of Maternal Charity, a private organization founded by Madame de Fougeret in 1784, placing it under the protection of the Empress and establishing a base fund of 500,000 francs in addition to any charitable contributions received. Aid was limited to married mothers having at least two young children living, or widows of veterans with at least one living child. While Madame de Fougeret's original society required its mothers to breast-feed their own infants in order to receive aid, "except in the case of absolute incapacity, duly documented" (Fuchs, 1992, 42–43),[7] the language of the Napoleonic decree seemed less strict in that regard: "[T]hese mothers will promise to nurse their babies themselves, or to raise their children on milk, if due to extraordinary circumstances they cannot nurse" (*Décret relatif à l'organisation de la charité maternelle*, 1843, 165).[8] While the type of milk (human, cow, goat) was not specified, the decree does insist on the idea of indigent women raising their own children rather than shipping them off to a distant wet nurse. It was less simple to impose such recommendations on wealthy women, however.

Napoleon's pragmatic repudiation of the glorification of the maternal body can also be seen in the replacement of the maternal figure of the Republic in the iconography of nationhood with the figure of Napoleon himself as the masculine embodiment of the Consular government and, later, the Empire.[9] As the well-endowed, bare-breasted Republic receded into the revolutionary past, to be revived at the rebirth of the French republic later in the nineteenth century, so did the popularity of breast-feeding imagery in general.

Legouvé and Chateaubriand: Motherhood in the Napoleonic Age

Let us look now at two examples of literary representations of breast-feeding from the Napoleonic period. The first is a hugely popular, twenty-five-page poem by Gabriel Legouvé, entitled *The Merits of Women*, first published in the year IX (1800–1801) and reprinted over forty times by 1899. Eugène Lesbazeilles wrote in 1886 that the poem was so much a part of popular culture in the early part of the century that "our grandmothers and our mothers knew [it] by heart" (1886, 343–44).[10]

In the tradition of the centuries-old *querelle des femmes* (quarrel about women), the poem begins with lengthy references to antiquity and the Bible, and then describes a young mother whose sole purpose in life is the care and feeding of her (male) infant:

> He wakes? her breast, presented right away,
> Bestows good health in waves of wholesome milk.
> What is fatigue to her boundless love?
> She lives for her son, no longer for herself;
> And shows herself to her ardent husband,
> Beautiful as she suckles the child at her breast.

> Yes, this fruit of marriage, this mother's gem,
> Is her main source of beauty, even to her. (Legouvé,
> 1800–1801, 22)[11]

This glorification of motherhood, with its portrayal of pure mother's milk flowing from an always instantly accessible breast, echoes the Rousseauist ideal of the nursing mother as portrayed in eighteenth-century literature and art. The last and most famous line of Legouvé's poem, "Fall at the feet of the sex to which you owe your mother!" (43),[12] also seems to perpetuate the glorification of motherhood that Rousseau had brought into fashion a half-century earlier. This line continued to echo through French literature for at least a century, as illustrated when Octave Mirbeau alluded to the line indirectly in a short story published in the periodical *L'Evènement* in the 1880s: "the sex to which I owe […] much less than I have given to it."[13]

However, these lines on motherhood represent only a small fraction of the poem and, despite their lyrical hyperbole and their popularity, they do not constitute the main theme of the work. In his preface, Legouvé, a Latin teacher and playwright and a regular in Josephine's *salon* during the consular period, explained his intentions quite clearly:

> When I composed this poem […] I intended, by outlining women's advantages, to bring back to their society a valorous people who have grown accustomed to distancing themselves from women due to the upheavals of the Revolution. In this way, I wanted to remind the people of their original courtesy, all but lost in the battles between parties. We must admit that the French had the graces of Athens, but now they have taken on a bit of the roughness of Sparta; and the example of those of our social climbers whose minds have been poorly educated, the influence of this new generation whose education was interrupted or altered by war, can increase from day to day this change in the national physiognomy. […] Ah! If the leaders of the Terror […] had appreciated women more, they would have spilled less blood; the man who cherishes them is rarely a barbarian. (Legouvé, 1800–1801, 15–16)[14]

To reinforce the political message of the civilizing influence of women, Legouvé included in the copious endnotes to his poem no fewer than thirty-five pages of anecdotes on the selfless bravery of women during the Terror who either saved their menfolk or insisted on being executed with them. One anecdote tells of Madame Elisabeth, the king's sister, who insisted on staying with the king when she could have escaped. When her shawl fell down as she was being led to the guillotine, her last words to the executioner were supposedly, "In the name of decency, cover my breast" (Legouvé, 1800–1801, 81).[15] Other anecdotes included women who saved their husbands, lovers, fathers, brothers, and even total strangers, but the author cited not a single example of maternal devotion, an omission that gives the lie to the famous last line of the poem. This text clearly did have a significant impact on its contemporaries; in fact, it was mainly due to the poem's critical and popular acclaim, aided perhaps by his acquaintance with Josephine, that Legouvé was elected to the Académie Française three years later. Despite the brief portrayal of the devoted nursing mother and the last line, however, the poem's post-revolutionary socio-political message had very little to do with motherhood.

Two years after the first edition of *The Merit of Women*, Chateaubriand published *The Genius of Christianism*, a defense of Christianity dedicated to First Consul Napoleon Bonaparte. In this work, the author cited the miracle of breast-feeding as evidence of the existence of God:

> The child is born, the breast is full; the young one has no teeth, so as not to harm the cup of the maternal banquet; he grows bigger, the milk becomes more nourishing; he is weaned; the amazing fountain dries up. (Chateaubriand, 1803, 260)[16]

He goes on to describe the incredible physical and moral feats of which a mother is capable on behalf of her young: "This weak woman has suddenly acquired a strength that makes her overcome fatigue that the most robust man could not withstand" (1803, 260).[17] For Chateaubriand, maternal instinct could only be a result of the Creator's handiwork: "From where does she get this ability that she had never had before? [...] Her caregiving seems to be the result of a lifetime of experience; and yet this is her firstborn!" (260–61).[18]

In contrast to his view of breast-feeding as innate and God-given, Chateaubriand's own mother sent him away to a wet nurse shortly after his birth. The author lamented his mother's absence in his memoirs in typically lyrical prose: "There is not a day when I do not revisit in my mind the rock on which I was born, the bedroom where my mother inflicted life on me [...] In leaving my mother's womb, I suffered my first exile. [...] Why did they not just let me die?" (Chateaubriand, 1948, vol. 1, pp. 30–32).[19] He attributed his survival to the prayers of his wet nurse and the resulting intervention of the Virgin Mary, "divine mother [...] sharing the solicitude of the earthly mother" (31).[20] He then attempts to justify his mother's apparent neglect: "My mother, by the way, full of wit and virtue, was busy with social activities and religious duties. [...] She loved politics, noise, society" (32).[21] This noble image of the virtuous, but ever-so-busy, mother is somewhat tarnished by the author's statement that his mother lavished all her available affection on her eldest son, while poor little François-René spent his youth "left to the servants' care" (32).[22] Chateaubriand embodies the lack of maternal care described by Allan Pasco, as does his hero René, from the novella published with *The Genius of Christianism*, whose story became the foundation of the tale of the Romantic hero in France.

In this context, the great majority of representations of breast-feeding in *The Genius of Christianism* depict not Frenchwomen but rather native American women, typically thought to be closer to nature than Europeans. *The Genius of Christianism* contains at least six lengthy descriptions of native American mothers either nursing a dead infant or putting their milk on an infant's grave. One native mother says to her dead child, "Oh! I must hurry to go find you again, to sing you songs, and give you my breast" (Chateaubriand, 1803, 267).[23] In *The Natchez,* after René's native American wife Céluta loses her milk, she wishes that she could nourish her child with tears, of which she has plenty; she then has the "deadly idea" ("funeste idée") of opening her veins to give her own blood to the baby in place of the milk she no longer has. Fortunately for her, as well as for her child, she is prevented from acting on this last impulse and finds a suitable wet nurse shortly thereafter.

While eighteenth-century authors tried to convince women to nurse for their own sakes, Chateaubriand's position seems to be that women in their natural state feel an overwhelming urge to nurse and to care for children, while women corrupted by society have lost this connection to their natural bodies. Paradoxically, however, according to the representations of "good" native mothers in Chateaubriand's works, not only are mothers who heed the call of nature no more likely to find happiness, but their devotion does not even guarantee their infants' survival. In a scene from *Atala,* the narrator describes a young native American mother by her infant's grave.

She sprinkled her milk over the ground; then, sitting on the damp grass, she spoke to her infant in a tender voice: "Why was I weeping for you in your earthen cradle, oh my newborn child! [...] At least you never knew sorrow; at least your heart was never exposed to the devouring breath of mankind. [...] Happy are those who die in the cradle, they have known only a mother's kisses and smiles!" (Chateaubriand, 1803, 194–95)[24]

The dead infant finds eternal happiness, or at least an eternal ignorance of sorrow, but what of the mother? In another chapter of *The Genius of Christianism*, Chateaubriand expresses pity for women who are destined to suffer through the loss of their children: "Woman renews her sorrows every time she becomes a mother, and she marries in tears. What suffering in the simple loss of a newborn to whom you give your milk, and who dies at your breast!" (1803, 249).[25] The link between cradle and tomb, between motherhood and sorrow, stands in sharp contrast to Greuze's happy mothers and children and Rousseau's ideal mother–child couple; although "natural" motherhood continues to be valorized, even the fierce protectiveness of the "natural" mother – the native American woman – cannot triumph over God's will. This morbid maternal devotion found a European echo a few years later in Germaine Necker de Staël's *On Germany*, when Staël quoted from Goethe's *Faust*, sharing with French readers the crazed Margaret's insistence on nursing her child after she had killed it (1958–60, 115).

Alice Weinreb has argued that, while images of breast-feeding Frenchwomen became less common in the age of Napoleon, French anxieties about the sexualization of the maternal body "were shifted away from France, and onto the breasts of the women of the New World" (2005, 19). While this idea may help to explain the paucity of white nursing mothers in popular literature and art during the Empire, it does not address the strange juxtaposition of lactation and death that marks *The Genius of Christianism*. This juxtaposition could be seen as an extension of the didactic paintings of the 1804 Salon, carrying a moral lesson on maternal devotion and on the price a mother must pay for failing to preserve her child's life. Moralists such as William Buchan and Duverne de Praile cited this exotic custom, which Chateaubriand calls "insane," in order to argue that, if native women could nurse in such extreme situations, privileged "civilized" women certainly could do so under normal circumstances (Burton,

2007, 66). In the epilogue to Chateaubriand's wildly popular novella *Atala*, we see the last surviving Natchez woman cradling her dead son, saying, "as my milk was bad, because of grief, it poisoned my baby" (1961, 273).[26] The failure of one mother to produce nourishing milk symbolized not only individual maternal suffering, but also the extinction of an entire race. Paradoxically, then, while Chateaubriand idealized the natural exotic maternal body in the abstract, his depictions of particular native American nursing mothers worked to resist this idealization by emphasizing the dysfunction and destructiveness of the nursing relationship, in much the same way that Napoleon's practical assessment of the maternal function undermined the glorification of the nursing breast.

Victor Hugo and the Price of Motherhood

In a poem written in 1837, entitled "Fiat voluntas" (Hugo, 1964, 1053–54), the Latin phrase for the biblical quote, "[God's] will be done," Victor Hugo tells the story of a nursing mother who goes insane at the death of her infant and finally dies as well. The poem begins: "Poor woman! Her milk has gone to her head" (1053),[27] describing her descent into insanity as a direct consequence of her abundance of milk: "she did not cry. Her milk and her fever / Suddenly made her head hurt and her lip tremble" (1053).[28] The mother's existence is represented as futile without the infant whose care gives her purpose: "Merciful God! What good is the mother's gaze without the sleeping child? What good is this white breast without that pink mouth?" (1964, 1053).[29] Most indicative of the misery brought on the nursing mother by the infant's death is the final stanza, which I will quote in its entirety:

> Lord! You have filled our world with mystery,
> In mankind, in love, in trees and in birds,
> And even in the milk claimed by a cradle,
> Ambrosia and poison, sweet honey, bitter liquid,
> Made to nourish the child or to kill the mother! (Hugo,
> 1964, 1054)[30]

Contrary to more traditional images of maternal milk as beneficial and life-giving, the milk itself becomes a poison, the agent of the mother's death. The poet speaks to a merciful God of the grieving mother's despair, which seems to be a natural force beyond her control. The poetic device of the mother's death by abundance of milk had a basis in medical beliefs of the day, which held that unused milk might be channeled to other parts of the anatomy, proving dangerous or even fatal to the mother (see Besnard, 1825). Here again we see the maternal instinct portrayed in a tragic and dysfunctional light, in contrast to the maternal bliss touted by moralists, painters, and novelists alike in the previous century.

In another poem, entitled "The Ghost" ("Le Revenant"), written six years later, Hugo returns to the theme of the grieving mother, with a very different dénouement. First, in a rhapsodic description reminiscent of earlier hymns to motherhood, we see the mother blissfully nursing her adored son:

> She leaned suddenly back in her chair,
> Her gown exposing her milk-swollen breast,
> And smiled at the weak infant, and called him
> Angel, treasure, love, and a thousand silly names.
> Oh! How she kissed those lovely little pink feet! (Hugo, 1922, 245)[31]

Then, the baby dies. We see the same symptoms of impending madness in the nursing mother: "She would not eat; her life was her fever; She responded to no one; her lip trembled" (245).[32] The doctor suggests to her husband that a new baby will cure her, and so she gets pregnant again; we are told that "she felt herself a mother for a second time" (245).[33] Still faithful to the memory of her dead son, she reluctantly allows the new baby to latch onto her breast, whereupon the baby murmurs softly to her: "It's me. Don't tell." (245).[34]

This spooky portrayal of reincarnation, manifested during the act of breast-feeding, restores the mother/son couple to its original bliss, but the purported "miracle" does not overshadow the bleak image of maternal suffering and despair throughout the poem. While the poem's opening lines alert the reader to the happy ending, they also warn of impending tragedy:

> Mourning mothers, your cries are heard on high.
> God, who holds all lost birds in His hand,
> Sometimes restores the same dove to the same nest.
> O mothers! The cradle is linked to the tomb. (Hugo, 1922, 245)[35]

The connection between cradle and tomb seems to evoke the issue of infant mortality, but this child's death, just as those of the infants in Chateaubriand, cannot be blamed on maternal neglect. These "good" mothers whose babies die despite their attentive care serve as examples, not of the proper behavior of mothers with their children, but rather of the effects of true maternal despair at the death of an infant. Like the native American women who sprinkled their dead infants' graves with milk, these mothers prove their maternal devotion by their lack of interest in a life without their infants. Their motherhood takes precedence over their selfhood, just as in the descriptions of the ideal mother in Rousseau; however, instead of glorifying this motherhood for its benefits to both mother and child, Chateaubriand and Hugo show us the dark side of maternal devotion, the ways in which mothers react to loss and grief.

Interestingly, however, in contrast to Chateaubriand, who spent his first three years with his *nourrice* in a distant village, Hugo was nursed by his mother. As he tells us in *Autumn Leaves*, published in 1831:

> Perhaps I will tell you one day
> How the pure milk, the caring, the wishes, the love
> Spent for my life, condemned at birth,
> Made me the child twice over of my stubborn mother.
> Oh mother love! Love that no one forgets!
> Marvelous bread that a god shares and multiplies! (Hugo, 1846, 14)[36]

Similarly, in an 1874 letter to his longtime mistress Juliette Drouet, he compares his mother's milk to Juliette's poetic inspiration: "I suckled from my mother who nursed me; I drank your soul on your lips, and you nursed me also, for you filled me with ideals" (Hugo, 1962, vol. 24, p. 248).[37] However, according to his biographers, Hugo was prone to bouts of melancholy from a very early age, beginning with his mother's trip to Paris without him when he was nine months old (see, for example, Richardson, 1976, 6). Despite Pasco's theories on the effects of maternal negligence on Romantic authors, it would seem that even dutiful breast-feeding mothers could produce melancholic, unfulfilled sons who write with longing of the maternal tenderness of their youth.

Lamartine and the "milk embittered with tears"

Like Victor Hugo, Alphonse de Lamartine, another iconic Romantic writer, was breast-fed by his loving mother during the days of the Revolution. In his autobiographical essay, *Confidences*, Lamartine tells the story of his early days with an emphasis on their political context and its influence on his generation. He describes the sudden unexplained imprisonment of his entire family, with the exception of his mother and himself:

> My father, through an exception whose cause he did not know, was separated from the rest of the family and locked up in the Macon prison. My mother, who was breast-feeding me at the time, was left alone in my grandfather's house, under the supervision of some soldiers of the Revolutionary army. And people are surprised that men whose lives began during those sinister days brought with them at birth a taste for sadness and an imprint of melancholy to French genius? Were not Virgil, Cicero, Tibullus, Horace himself, who imprinted this charac-teristic onto Roman genius, born, like us, during the great civil wars of Rome and within earshot of the proscriptions of Marius, Scylla, and Caesar? Think of the impressions of terror or pity that agitated the entrails of Roman women while they were carrying these men in their wombs! Think of the milk embittered by tears that I myself received from my mother while the entire family was in a captivity that could end only in death! (Lamartine, 1879, 36–37)[38]

By constructing a parallel between a list of Roman writers beloved by the previous generation of classicism and the Romantic authors of his generation in France, Lamartine bestows historical legitimacy on the melancholy known as the *mal du siècle*, the longing for a better life that Allan Pasco has attributed to these authors' early separation anxiety from their neglectful mothers. Lamartine's mother did not fit Pasco's model, however; she continued to nurse him despite her distress, feeding the infant in front of her husband's prison window:

> My poor mother carried me in her arms ever day to the attic, showed me to my father, breast-fed me in front of him, had me reach toward the prison bars with my tiny hands; then, pressing

my forehead to her chest, she covered me with kisses, thus addressing to the prisoner all the caresses that she bestowed on me but that were intended for him. (Lamartine, 1879, 40–41)[39]

Baby Alphonse and his mother spent eighteen months awaiting the judgment and inevitable execution of the prisoners, but to their surprise, his father and other relatives were liberated following the overthrow of Robespierre on the 9th of Thermidor (1879, 45). As he grew into a man and became the Romantic poet and politician with whom we are familiar, Lamartine continued to be close to his mother until her death in 1829, eleven days after her son's election to the French Academy.

In the years following her death, Lamartine wrote *Jocelyn*, an epic poem whose seventh part constituted an elegy to the author's mother in the words of the title character. Critic Henri Guillemin notes the similarities between the descriptions of Jocelyn's childhood here and what we know of Lamartine's life, including the location, the portrayal of the loving and doting mother, and his affection for dogs. The poem even echoes a letter from the author to the Princess Borghese on the day after his mother's death (1936, 409–11). In the text, Jocelyn remembers his mother while visiting her tomb:

> I loved her, but in loving her was I not a part of her?
> Was I not nourished by the milk from her breast,
> Hatched from her love, warmed in her womb,
> The marrow of her bones, the purest of her blood?
> Was not the air she breathed in her chaste bosom
> For nine months the same that my nostrils breathed?
> Did her heart, next to mine, not inspire with each beat
> The same sentiment in my heart made complete?
> Was my body not her entire body, and my soul
> A borrowed hearth lit by another flame? (Lamartine, 1860,
> vol. 4, p. 335)[40]

This passionate union between mother and son echoes the passage of Lamartine's *Confidences*: "[O]ther mothers only carried their child for nine months in their womb; I can say that mine carried me for twelve years, and that I lived her moral life as I had lived her physical life in her womb, up to the moment when I was torn from her to go live the putrid or at least glacial life of boarding school" (1879, 41–42).[41]

On the surface, Lamartine would seem to contradict Pasco's theory on the influence of maternal neglect, and more specifically the custom of wet-nursing, on the Romantic psyche. However, it is interesting to note that with the exception of *Jocelyn*, Lamartine's body of work holds few representations of nursing mothers. For critic Sébastien Baudoin, Lamartine's lifelong adoration of his mother as his muse and his inspiration merely gave the author another way of talking about himself, a characteristic trait of Romantic writers, through the "mediation of the image of his mother's womb" (2016, 217). His references to his mother's milk "embittered with tears" could be read as an extension of his melancholic self, the original source of the *mal du siècle* embedded in most Romantic literature and in the story of the Romantic hero. If the maternal breast plays a role in Lamartine's work, it is one of creation, its significance resting entirely in the future destiny of the male child. Like Hugo and Chateaubriand, Lamartine bestows on the nursing mother the task of nurturing the hero, while downplaying the elements of grief and mourning that mark so much of Chateaubriand's and Hugo's work. Still, Lamartine's mother gave him milk mixed with tears, the ideal nourishment for a future Romantic poet.

Breast-Feeding in Paintings of the Early 1800s

Art historian Kathryn Calley-Galitz has documented a decrease after 1800 in the number of nursing mothers represented in the official exhibits of paintings and sculptures, or *salons*. According to Calley-Galitz, "[t]he political content inherent in images of maternal breast-feeding produced during the Republic was replaced with a didacticism intent on restricting woman's maternal role to the private sphere, reflecting the increasing patriarchal emphasis of the Napoleonic regime" (1998, 30). While this didacticism resembles in many ways that of the eighteenth-century "happy mother" imagery described by Carol Duncan, I argue that the visual art of the post-revolutionary period seems to forego the blissful maternal scenes of Greuze in order to highlight the negative example of the non-nursing, or non-productive, maternal body. This is illustrated by three sets of images by women artists, Marguerite Gérard, Henriette Lorimier, and Constance Mayer, all protégées of the empress Josephine, from the first decade of the century.

In the Salon of 1804, Marguerite Gérard, student and sister-in-law of Fragonard, presented two paintings considered by critics as a thematic pair: "A Nursing Mother Presenting Her Breast To Her Child, Brought To Her By A Governess"[42] and "A Child Brought by his Wet Nurse to his Mother, Whom He Refuses to Recognize" (Calley-Galitz, 1998, 30).[43] In the first work, we see a serene and welcoming maternal figure toward whom the toddler reaches hungrily as she offers him one bared breast in readiness to nurse. The mother gazes affectionately at the child, whose eagerness is evident in his outstretched hand and his gaze locked with hers. The second, according to critics at the time, portrayed a child's preference for his wet nurse over his mother. One contemporary critic wrote of the second of these two moralistic paintings: "Perhaps it will also strengthen the resolve of some young wife … May she accept the advice given by this painting – think of all the tears she will spare herself! It must be a cruel torture for a mother to see her child, from its cradle, giving the lie to nature" (30).[44] The same Salon (1804) also featured a similar painting by Joseph Flouest, *A Child Brought Back from the Wet-Nurse Who Refuses His Mother's Embrace*.[45] Here the child twists and writhes in his effort to escape his mother's arms, despite the restraining hand of the father and the admonishing gesture of the wet nurse. This subject, with its moralizing message, was common in the 1770s and 1780s as well, as in *Adieux to the Wet-Nurse* by Étienne Aubry, from 1776. However, the child's sadness at leaving his wet nurse in the Aubry painting contrasts sharply with the clearly hysterical distress of the child in the 1804 Flouest painting, further enhancing the underlying message of maternal inadequacy and guilt.

Ironically, however, the painting on infant feeding that attracted the most critical attention at the 1804 Salon did not involve a human breast at all: Henriette Lorimier's *A Young Woman Watching A Goat Nurse Her Child*. The full description in the catalogue read: "A young woman. Not having been able to nurse her child, she watches him nursing from the goat that stands in for her and she lets herself ponder the thoughts that her situation evokes" (Denton, 1998, 245 n. 91).[46] Critics praised the artist for choosing a subject appropriate to her sex and pitied the young mother for her inability to produce milk, citing "the injustice of nature" in depriving her of her "sacred rights" (Calley-Galitz, 1998, 30–31). One male critic assumed the voice of the mother in the painting saying to her child: "Alas, my child, despite this lovely breast that I am showing you, nature has denied me the pleasure of being able to nurse you! How I envy the happiness of this goat. I am in a stable, it's true, but I am there with my child" (Denton, 1998, 245 n. 93).[47] Clearly the glorification of the mother has faded, along with the voyeuristic pleasure of representing, and viewing, the nursing breast. Due to the great success of this first painting, Lorimier painted a sequel, entitled *The Grateful Child* that appeared in the Salon in 1810 and again in 1814 (Calley-Galitz, 1998, 32).

Constance Mayer, student of first Greuze and then Prud'hon, produced two paintings, *The Happy Mother* and *The Unfortunate Mother*, which appeared as *pendants* in the Salons of both 1810 and 1814, testifying to their popularity and their accordance with contemporary ideals, if not actual practice. *The Happy Mother* shows a mother who has just nursed her sleeping child. The idyllic forest setting and the mother's attire, in particular her bare feet, bring to mind Rousseau's injunctions on the laws of nature that directed mothers to nurse their children. The large-breasted mother gazes adoringly at the sleeping child, while a soft sunlight illuminates the clearing where she sits. The other painting, *The Unfortunate Mother*, shows a thin, flat-chested, miserable-looking woman in a similar (but darker) forest setting, pining for her dead child, whose tomb we see at the bottom right. Taken as a thematic pair, these paintings tell a clear story of good and bad motherhood that was reinforced by the reactions of the critics. Landon wrote in *Annales du salon:* "A young woman who has lost her child has built a tomb for him in a solitary valley. A stone, covered with moss and grass and topped with a cross with a crown of roses hanging from it, forms the modest monument of maternal love. The unfortunate mother contemplates the spot where the remains of her beloved one lie, with a painful expression and with eyes bathed in tears" (Landon, 1810, 23).[48] Apart from the obvious moral lesson on the maternal duty to breastfeed, these paintings create an aesthetic contrast between maternal happiness and misery that echoes the conflict in maternal representations throughout this period. A mother's sublime joy can quickly turn to deep despair, in other words, if her child is taken from her.

Of these images, only the first one by Gérard represented a nursing mother with an exposed breast, in contrast to the numerous examples of bare-breasted nursing mothers in Salon paintings, mostly by men, from 1780 to 1800. In her thesis on women artists during this period, Margaret Oppenheimer noted that "apart from the work of Marguerite Gerard, who is virtually the only woman specializing in scenes of mothers and children before 1802, there are hardly any women in the Revolutionary and Empire periods who specialize in scenes of maternity and family life" (1996, 299). Since Gérard, Mayer, and Lorimier had no children of their own, their representations were necessarily based, not on lived experience, but on observation and ideology. What interests me here, however, is the way in which the voyeuristic quality of earlier representations, mostly by male artists, complete with frontal nudity, is replaced by an emphasis on the non-nursing maternal body and its didactic function as a cautionary tale. The body of the non-nursing mother and her son's rejection of that body serve as a warning to women, and to the viewing public in general, of the possible consequences of women's departure from traditional motherhood.

George Sand's Representation of the Nursing Peasant Mother: Exception to the Rule

Aurore Dupin, known by her *nom de plume*, George Sand, began a prolific career as a novelist in the early 1830s that continued right up to her death in 1876. Many of her novels represented the peasants and the customs of the Berry, the French province where Sand spent much of her childhood. Drawing from her observations of peasant culture as well as from her own experience, Sand created representations of both nursing mothers and wet nurses in her novels. Sand's family had a long tradition of breast-feeding; her grandmother and her mother had nursed their own children, the grandmother by conviction after reading Rousseau, as we saw in Chapter 1, and her mother most likely for economic reasons. As Sand wrote matter-of-factly in her autobiography, *Story of my Life*, "My mother had never read Jean-Jacques Rousseau and may not even have heard much about him, but that did not keep her from breast-feeding me, just as she had done and would do for all her other children" (1879, vol. 40, p. 80).[49] When Sand had her own children (Maurice in 1823 and Solange in 1828), she breast-fed them as a matter of course, despite the prevailing trend of hiring a wet nurse, and without fanfare or justification: "I breast-fed my son, just as I later did with his sister" (1879, vol. 41, p. 436).[50]

Having the experience of breast-feeding her own children, Sand, unlike the male authors of her time, had the advantage of her own observations to draw from when creating fictional characters who might lactate. Breast-feeding in Sand's work mostly appears as a normal part of life, without any special emotional or psychological significance, and is occasionally mentioned in passing, when it is mentioned at all. In *La Petite Fadette* (1849), Mother Barbeau gives birth to twins and ignores the midwife's advice to have them drink different milk. In a skillfully reasoned argument to convince her husband not to send one of the twins to a wet nurse, she uses financial and health concerns:

> Bah! Husband, I don't see why we should spend 180 or 200 pounds per year, as if we was lords and ladies, and as if I was too old to feed my kids. I have more than enough milk for that. They're a month old already, our boys, and look at what good shape they're in! Merlaud's wife, who you want to hire as a wet nurse for one of them, is not half as strong or as healthy as me; her milk is already eighteen months old, and that's not what such a young baby needs. (Sand, 1857b, vol. 6, p. 561)[51]

After the husband reluctantly agrees, the narrator tells us that Mother Barbeau breast-fed her two twins "without complaint and without suffering" and then proceeded to nurse her next baby as well, with occasional help from her eldest daughter who was then nursing her first child (1857b, vol. 6, p. 561).[52]

In another scene, from the novel *Horace* (1842), Marthe does her best to breast-feed her illegitimate infant in conditions of abject poverty:

> The child was the only one who did not suffer too much from this distress. His mother did not have much milk; but the neighbor shared the milk from her breakfast with the newborn, and every day she carried him in her arms as she strolled in the sun on the Quai of Flowers. That is all a Parisian child needs to grow like a frail but tenacious plant. (Sand, 1857a, 308)[53]

The baby thrives, despite the terrible conditions and his mother's lack of milk, without much fuss, thanks to the help of the kindly neighbor. His good health becomes a symbol of the toughness and tenacity of Parisian youth.

The wealthy former actress in *Lucrezia Floriani* (1857) tells us that she nursed all four of her children herself, both before and after her retirement from the stage.

My children never had any other wet nurse but me, and the first two often suckled from my breast offstage, between two scenes. I remember one time the audience was calling me back with such despotism after the first play that I was forced to take a bow with my baby under my shawl. (Sand, 1880, 57)[54]

Lucrezia presents breast-feeding as a practical necessity that she carried out while working as an actress. She seems to take it in stride as a normal part of motherhood, which contrasts to the strong preference of most mothers of the time with means to hire a wet nurse.

Overall, the handful of representations of maternal breast-feeding in Sand's novels seem to be less metaphorical and dramatic and more matter-of-fact than those in the works of other authors of this period. Sand presented breast-feeding, like childbirth, as a vital task that must be performed to preserve the health of a newborn, and Sand's characters generally went about nursing (or hiring a wet nurse when needed) without further ado, much as she did in real life. We can see this pragmatic attitude in a letter to her husband Casimir of July 29, 1823, when she was nursing their son: "Your little angel Maurice slept well last night, nursed well this morning, peed and pooped well, etc." (1964, vol. 1, p. 108).[55] Here, nursing becomes part of a list of essential but uninteresting bodily functions of normal infants. In sharp contrast to Lamartine's mother's "milk embittered with tears" or Chateaubriand's native American women dousing their infants' graves with their own breast milk, Sand's characters approached breast-feeding much as Sand herself did, removing the pathos and moral overtones in favor of brief but accurate descriptions of practical details.

In her allegorical novel *Isidora*, published in 1845, Sand's title character shares this judgement of Rousseau with Jacques, the narrator: "He did not understand women, the sublime Rousseau. [...] The most spiritualist of the philosophers was materialist when it came to women" (1861, 33).[56] Through the voice of her title character, Sand accused Rousseau of materialism, of valuing women's breasts and their nutritive function over the more spiritual formation of mothers who would both love and nurture their children. Yet it is that very function, with all its physicality, that Sand privileged in her few portrayals of nursing mothers. Lyrical praise of breast-feeding as a sign of maternal love seems to be absent from Sand's fiction. Perhaps that explains why she bestowed such effusive praise on her friend and correspondent Honoré de Balzac for his representation of the nursing mother in *Memoirs of Two Young Married Women*, as we will see in the next chapter.

In this analysis of breast-feeding in Romantic imagery, we have seen evidence of a trend away from the earlier glorification of the maternal breast promoted by Rousseau and his disciples. As Napoleon strove to create an empire based on masculine virtues, the mother's role shrank from that of adored and nurturing caregiver, source of all life, to that of a breeder at the service of the nation. The emperor's initiatives to improve midwifery training in France could also be seen as a consequence of this shift in importance from the producer (the mother) to the product (the child and future citizen/soldier). In an explanation of the rights of husbands, as laid out in the Napoleonic Code, to control both their wives' bodies and their children, Napoleon said: "Woman is given to man so she can make babies for him. She is therefore his property like the fruit tree is that of the gardener" (Burton, 2007, 6).[57] While the fruit tree should be protected and provided for, there is no question of worshiping it or of crediting it with the reformation of the French nation. Once the maternal body has fulfilled its essential and eminently practical function, it should disappear back into the private sphere where it belongs, leaving the public sphere of empire to men.

For similar reasons, perhaps Napoleon's post-exile body, confined entirely to the private sphere by his forced exclusion from political and public life, could safely be feminized, since it no longer functioned as a symbol of masculine power or of nationhood. In *Le Mémorial de Sainte-Hélène*, an account of Napoleon's years in his final exile, Las Cases describes Napoleon as "quite stout, not very hairy, with white skin and a certain roundness that is not typical of our sex, a fact he comments on gaily from time to time" (1812, vol. 1, p. 423).[58] Just as the imperial breasts would stay safely tucked away in the private sphere, so should those of the mother. Like Napoleon's penis, which supposedly resides in a tasteful case of Moroccan leather in an attic in New Jersey, the maternal breast would remain, for the duration of the Empire and for most of the Romantic period, safely in the closet (Perrottet, 2008, 22).

Chapter 3

Realism, Naturalism, and the
Eroticization of Breast-Feeding

In 1898, Dr. Gustave Joseph Witkowski described a peculiar phenomenon: "Certain lactating women, hysterics for example, experiencing a special enjoyment in the titillations of the nipple, prolong breast-feeding to the extreme. Dr. Jose de Letamendi noted this vice […] and gave it the name of mastomania or sensual breast-feeding" (1898, 67). The concept of sexual pleasure while breast-feeding, still faintly scandalous in the twenty-first century, circulates in a variety of French cultural productions from the mid- to the late nineteenth century, from medical discourse to the fictional works of Balzac, Flaubert, and Zola. In such representations, it is often the male gaze that constructs meaning by either reaffirming the pleasures of nursing for the sake of the infant or revealing a desire to take the place of the child.

One example can be seen in Flaubert's early autobiographical work, *Memoirs of a Crazy Man*, written in 1838 but not published until 1900:

> Maria had a child, it was a little girl […] Maria was breast-feeding her herself, and one day, I saw her uncover her bosom and offer the child her breast. It was a fat and round bosom, with brown skin and azure veins that could be seen in that ardent flesh. I had never seen a naked woman then. Oh! The singular ecstasy I felt upon seeing that breast; how I devoured it with my eyes, how I would have wished to merely touch that bosom! It seemed to me that if I had placed my lips upon it, my teeth would have bitten it furiously, and my heart melted in delight as I thought about the

Versions of portions of this chapter were published previously in the *Journal of the Motherhood Initiative* (Toronto) 7.2 (2017) and in *Romance Studies* 32.1 (2014).

sensual pleasure such a kiss would give me. Oh! How often I have imagined that palpitating bosom. (Flaubert, 2014, 37)[1]

The fifteen-year-old male narrator indicates without ambiguity the sexual attraction of the maternal breast and its power over his psyche even years later. The reciprocal desire of mother and infant shifts to include a third party, the male spectator, whose own desire for the breast creates a fantasy of maternal erotic response to the nursling. This confusion of subject and object of desire raises complex questions about the motivations of the male authors of these texts. In this chapter, I will argue that the erotic dimension of the breast-feeding mother was tolerated, and even celebrated, in nineteenth-century French realism, but only when the male gaze constructed and controlled the mother's desire.

Breast-Feeding, Eroticism, and the Male Gaze

Although it may seem oddly modern in the twenty-first century, the idea of sensual breast-feeding was far from new in the nineteenth century; as we saw in Chapter 1, prior to the Enlightenment, medical authorities in France such as Laurent Joubert and Ambroise Paré saw sexual stimulation while breast-feeding as nature's way of enticing women to nurse. In their view, wealthy mothers who hired a wet nurse were overlooking a source of potential pleasure. Joubert wrote in 1578 that "if they [mothers] knew what pleasure there is in nursing children, which wet nurses enjoy, they would praise them for nursing other people's children, rather than abandoning their own" (Joubert, 1578, 418). According to Valerie Lastinger, this matter-of-fact acceptance of maternal arousal became more problematic after the Enlightenment's definition of motherhood carefully segregated the maternal and the sexual: "the sexual element of the nursing couple's bonding was not one that the encyclopedists discussed, or even mentioned, and it soon became taboo" (1996, 611).

One of the consequences of this separation of the maternal and the sexual, as philosopher Iris Marion Young has noted, was that it increased woman's dependence on man for sexual gratification. As Young explains, "If motherhood is sexual, the mother and child can be a circuit of pleasure for the mother, then the man may lose her allegiance and attachment [...] she may find him dispensable" (1990, 198–99). Seen in this light, segregating mothers from the possibility of sexual pleasure in the mother–child relationship is a strategy for controlling female sexuality.

In his treatise on education, *Émile*, published in 1762, Enlightenment philosopher Jean-Jacques Rousseau described maternal breast-feeding as the "sweet task imposed on [mothers] by nature" (1921, 14). In Rousseau's worldview, the act of nursing one's child represented a duty rather than a pleasure, and he noted the benefits to the nursing mother mostly in terms of the moral and social advantages. In fact, he warned that the "violence of the passions" could spoil a woman's milk (24). Rousseau included a vague reference to the "pleasures associated by nature with maternal duties" (24) but gave no indication as to what those pleasures might be. For him, mothers should nurse their children to reform society and improve morals, not for their own selfish gain.

By 1802, the subject of maternal pleasure while breast-feeding had been relegated to a mere footnote. In his medical treatise on the relationship between the physical and the moral, Dr. Cabanis wrote: "Several nursing mothers have confessed to me that the child suckling them made them feel a strong sensation of pleasure, shared to some degree by the reproductive organs. Other women have told me also that often the joys or pains of motherhood were accompanied by a state of orgasm of the uterus" (1844, 250). Despite Lastinger's assertions of the influence of the encyclopedists on maternal sexuality, however, the idea of sexual pleasure while nursing does appear in select literary texts throughout the nineteenth century, often with the addition of a male spectator. In order to analyze the importance of the male gaze to these representations, we need to first examine basic theories of psychoanalysis on mothering and sexuality, from Freud to Kristeva.

Psychoanalytic Theory and Maternal Sexuality

Sigmund Freud, the father of modern psychology, saw the infant as a solution to maternal penis envy. For Freud, this substitution naturally led to the mother's treatment of the child as object of desire. Freud argued that "the person in charge of him [the child], who, after all, is as a rule his mother, herself regards him with feelings that are derived from her own sexual life: she strokes him, kisses him, rocks him and quite clearly treats him as a substitute for a complete sexual object" (1989, 288–89). Post-Freudian feminist psychoanalysts, however, have challenged this idea as originating more in the male gaze of the analyst than in the female psyche. As Luce Irigaray puts it, "Woman, in this sexual imaginary, is a more or less complacent facilitator for the working out of man's fantasies" (1980, 100). However, although she objected to Freud's phallocentrism, Irigaray did not deny the ambiguity of maternal sexuality in a patriarchal society:

> In her relation to the child [the mother] finds compensatory pleasure for the frustrations she encounters all too often in sexual relations proper. Thus, maternity supplants the deficiencies of repressed female sexuality. [...] Man, identified with his son, rediscovers the pleasure of maternal coddling; woman retouches herself in fondling that part of her body: her baby-penis-clitoris. (Irigaray, 1980, 102)

In this model, then, maternal breast-feeding provides sexual gratification for both sexes: for the woman through her child's caresses, and for the man through a regressive identification with the (presumed male) nursling. Freud articulated this identification as well as the voyeuristic element in his description of the infant's sexual satisfaction: "No one who has seen a baby sinking back satiated from the breast and falling asleep with flushed cheeks and a blissful smile can escape the reflection that this picture persists as a prototype of the expression of sexual satisfaction in later life" (1949, 60). For Freud, the (male) infant's sexual gratification took center stage and formed the basis for much of Freud's later theories on sexual instinct. The mother's sexualization of the nursing relationship was a secondary result of the mother's frustration at not having a penis.

Building on Freud's theories of infant development, Melanie Klein described the process of projective identification of the infant with the mother, which involved the infant projecting parts of its ego into the mother. Although this type of identification could lead to the rejection of the mother along with the bad ego parts of the infant, it also promoted the infant's interdependence with the mother (Likierman, 2001, 157–60). This identification of the infant with its mother, or more specifically with its mother's breast, could also be a source of unconscious anxiety centered on the maternal figure. As Klein argued, "The phantasy of forcefully entering the object gives rise to anxieties relating to the dangers threatening the subject from within the object, that is, the fear of being controlled and persecuted inside the object" (1946, 11). This suggested a link between male anxiety and the perception of the mother's breast and may help explain some of the ambiguity in the male spectator's interpretation of the mother–infant relationship

According to Julia Kristeva, since maternal *jouissance* (a French word meaning both orgasm and enjoyment) represents a threat to the social order of procreation required by a modern bourgeois economy, mothers must seek fulfillment through another kind of jouissance centered in the maternal experience. Kristeva writes:

> the fact that the mother is other, has no penis, but experiences jouissance and bears children [...] is acknowledged only at the pre-conscious level: just enough to imagine that she bears children, while censuring the fact that she has experienced jouissance in an act of coitus, that there was a "primal scene." Once more, the vagina and the jouissance of the mother are disregarded, and immediately replaced by that which puts the mother on the side of the socio-symbolic community: childbearing and procreation in the name of the Father. (Kristeva, 1986, 146–47)

This displacement of maternal jouissance from vaginal intercourse to the pleasures of procreation authorizes women to find pleasure in maternal activities such as breast-feeding, but only if they are performed "in the name of the Father," within the controlled heteronormative framework of patriarchy.

Balzac, Zola, and the Return of the Erotic Maternal Breast

The male subjugation of maternal desire is apparent in literary representations of the mother–infant couple in nineteenth-century France. Honoré de Balzac's *Memoirs of Two Young Married Women*, an epistolary novel published in 1841, tells the story of two girls who meet in convent school and their very different destinies—Renée and Louise each represent a different side of women's lives. Renée enters into a loveless marriage and places all her hopes on the joys of motherhood, whereas Louise pursues romantic love through two marriages, only to despair in the end at her continued sterility. As Renée writes "We are born to privileges; we can choose between love and motherhood. Well, I have chosen; I shall make my gods my children" (Balzac, 1894, 67). The usual platitudes describing motherhood as the ultimate reward of women traverse the novel, making Louise feel more and more inadequate in comparison to her friend's blooming maternal bliss. Renée writes of her future children: "I can … find my life in theirs" (or, in the original French, "je jouirai de la vie par eux") (1976, vol. 1, p. 112). Although Balzac's use of the verb *jouir*, which can mean "to enjoy" or in some contexts "to orgasm," may appear innocent here, it seems reasonable to read more into this turn of phrase than the surface meaning indicates in light of later sexual descriptions of Renée's sensations while nursing,

As in Kristeva's model of maternal jouissance, Renée's sexuality is focused on an alternative mode of pleasure, one linked to the maternal body. Her expectations of motherhood subtly reflect this displaced sexuality:

> Maternity is an enterprise in which I have opened an enormous credit; it owes me so much that I fear it can never pay me in full; it is charged with developing my energy, enlarging my heart, and compensating me for all things by illimitable joys. Oh! my God, grant that I not be defrauded! There lies all my future, and – oh, terrifying thought! – my virtue. (Balzac, 1894, 135)

Although the exact nature of the "illimitable joys" that she expects is unclear, what does seem clear is that her virtue depends on her maternal fulfillment; she therefore sees this fulfillment as an equal to, and indeed a sufficient substitute for, sexual relations with a man.

Many scholars have opposed the two main characters, Renée and Louise, as embodiments of duty versus passion, or passionless motherhood versus sensually fulfilled sterility. Contemporary critics saw Balzac's novel, particularly the ending, where Louise dies, as "a resounding denial of the new theories on woman's independence, and a work written for moral purposes."[2] More recent critics often agree with this sentiment, though they might grant the novel more complexity surrounding women's issues. Max Andréoli, writing in 1987, concluded that the only path to salvation for women according to this novel lay in marriage and conjugal love, portrayed as "a life devoid of all fervor and all passion" (1987, 272).[3] In 1996, André Lorant put it even more succinctly: "Louise the orgasmic is compared to Renée who has never had an orgasm" (1996, 292).[4]

I argue that while Renée's conjugal relationship may be devoid of true passion, her experience of motherhood becomes a source of sexual gratification for her that rivals Louise's satisfaction from her scandalous affairs. In his 1981 preface to the novel, Bernard Pingaud hinted at this parallel when he wrote that Renée sought in motherhood "a substitute for pleasure" and called Renée's experience "as sensually rich as the one Louise prides herself on" (Balzac, 1981, 16–18).[5] Ye Young Chung, in a 2005 article, noted more explicitly the mix of the maternal and the sexual in this novel. According to Chung, each character assumes a stereo-typical role, either mother or courtesan, both of which are "projections of masculine fantasies" whose characteristics are understood from the outset (2005, 340).[6] However, these characters make those roles their own: "even if the woman is imprisoned in the maternal space created by masculine discourse, the corporeal experience transgresses that space, and at the same time the patriarchal space" (340).[7] The sexual nature of Renée's maternal pleasure becomes most evident in her descriptions of the experience of nursing her first child (not surprisingly, a son). Here, the representation of erotic pleasure is unmistakable:

> The little monster took my breast and sucked: there, there was the fiat lux! Suddenly, I was a mother. [...] The little being knows absolutely nothing but our breast. [...] His lips are love inexpressible, and when they fasten there they cause both pain and pleasure, pleasure which stretches into pain, pain which ends in pleasure. I cannot explain to you a sensation which radiates from my bosom to the sources of life; it seemed that a thousand rays start from that center to rejoice both heart and soul. To bear a child is nothing; to suckle it, nourish it, is to bear it for all time. Oh! Louise! there are no caresses of any lover that can equal that of the little rosy fingers which move so softly trying to clutch at life. (Balzac, 1894, 192)[8]

This passage is Renée's direct response to Louise's insistence in the previous letter that "[i]f I am to know nothing of the joys of motherhood, you will tell them to me; and I shall be a mother through you; but in my opinion there can be nothing comparable to the delights of love" (Balzac, 1894, 186). Renée describes a pleasurable feeling that moves from her breast to the "sources of life," referring to her womb, a clear indication of sexual or at least sensual pleasure while breast-feeding. Her direct comparison between the feeling of her child's fingers on her breast and the touch of a lover further sexualizes the breast-feeding couple, with the infant son serving as an erotic surrogate for the lover/ father figure. This extraordinary passage, unique in French literature up to that point, portrays the orgasmic experience of breast-feeding in a way that no other author, male or female, had previously done. How did Balzac know such details about the breast-feeding experience, and why did he choose to portray it in this way?

Other scholars have remarked on the extraordinary ability of Balzac to get inside the skin of the maternal body. Philippe Berthier, in a 2005 article, calls *Memoirs of Two Young Married Women* "a feminine novel – a truly transsexual text in which a mind manages to not only enter into another's body [...] but, considerably more difficult, to enter into a female other's body" (2005, 305).[9] Berthier describes the extreme physicality of the stages of motherhood as seen in the novel, from gestation to childbirth to breast-feeding, as a rare effort on the part of a male author, remarkable for both its audacity and its honesty (302). While most critics underline the lack of sexual fulfillment in Renée's marriage as compared to her friend Louise's libidinal adventures, Berthier emphasizes the erotic aspect of Renée's immersion in motherhood.

> As much as is possible for him, Balzac puts himself in the skin of a breast-feeding woman and fantasizes himself with swollen breasts, inexhaustible, sensual – for there again it is all about an erotic euphoria. If she doesn't experience the same intoxications as her friend Louise in Macumer's arms, Renée still wants her to know that she has access to another mode of pleasure, which is unimaginable to someone who is only a lover. (Berthier, 2005, 302)[10]

Although Renée's alternative mode of pleasure (Berthier used the verb *jouir*) originates in the physical sensations of breast-feeding, the suggestion that the male author fantasizes his own body as female reinforces the concept of male breast-feeding fantasy at the heart of this representation of the lactating body.

Berthier's critique echoes the words of Henry James, in his preface to the 1902 translation of *The Two Young Brides*: "He gets, for further intensity, into the very skin of his *jeunes mariées* ..." (Balzac, 1902, xlii). For James, however, Balzac takes on both the maternal persona and that of the child. "He bears children with Mme. de l'Estorade, knows intimately how she suffers for them, and not less intimately how her correspondent suffers, as well as enjoys, without them. Big as he is he makes himself small to be handled by her with young maternal passion and positively to handle her in turn with infantile innocence" (xlii). Balzac the infant puts himself in the place of the infant being handled by its mother "with young maternal passion," which reminds us of the orgasmic breast-feeding scene quoted above, as well as "to handle her in turn," evoking the caress of the male infant's little rosy fingers on the mother's breast.

James described Balzac's great gift as "a kind of shameless personal, physical, not merely intellectual, duality – the very spirit and secret of transmigration" (xliii). Transmigration, also known as metempsychosis, is the belief that the soul can migrate into another body after death.[11] Balzac's ability to transport himself into the physical body of a woman (or, indeed, of anyone, as James wrote) seemed to James the secret to the intensity of his representations, next to which other types of representation feel "so void of the active contortions of truth as to be comparatively wooden" (xlii). Similarly, George Sand, to whom Balzac dedicated the novel, wrote to him in February of 1842: "[M]y dear, you must have had a previous existence in which you were a woman and a mother, following the ideas of Leroux.[12] After all, you know so many things that no one knows" (Balzac, 2017, vol. 3, p. 18).[13] Sand's implication is that no one who is male could possibly know such things unless he had lived a former existence as a woman. James, apparently, agreed with her.

In her 2001 book on childhood in nineteenth-century France, social historian Catherine Rollet noted the originality of Balzac's portrayal of breast-feeding in the novel:

> Balzac, in a passage of *Memoirs of Two Young Married Women*, surprises the reader by the modernity of his remarks on the breast-feeding experience. He takes pleasure in describing the joys of breast-feeding, physical and psychic joys mixed together. [...] One could not describe this pleasure of breast-feeding any better, for both the baby and the mother, pleasure that, according to Balzac, makes a woman a mother and competes with sexual pleasure. This novel is written in 1841, and only rarely will other authors in the second half of the century celebrate breast-feeding with such lyricism. (Rollet, 2001, 32)[14]

Rollet points out that while Balzac's Renée finds nursing both pleasurable and fulfilling, later portrayals by Zola and others emphasize the primary importance of the baby's well-being over the mother's. Despite the hyperbolic lyrical praise of the nursing mother Marianne in Zola's *Fécondité*, which we will examine later, breast-feeding becomes less of a joy of motherhood and more of a duty prescribed by doctors in the fifty years separating the two novels, according to Rollet.

Roger Pierrot, in his 1976 preface to *Memoirs of Two Young Married Women*, identified two possible sources for Balzac's intimate acquaintance with the experience of motherhood – his sister Laure Surville and his close friend Zulma Carraud (Balzac, 1976, vol. 1, p. 178). According to Pierrot, "Renée as a mother is Zulma. [...] Thanks to the written and spoken confidences of Zulma Carraud, he was able to transpose his own sensibility and describe the joys and the pains of motherhood, as doubtless no other man had ever done" (vol. 1, pp. 187–88).[15] In 1983, Raymond Trousson claimed that Carraud, an attentive mother, inspired Balzac's portrait of the maternal Renée, which made her seem "infinitely more real" than Rousseau's Julie (1983, 231). On June 9, 1834, Carraud wrote to Balzac: "You will never know what it is to be a mother; that privilege of motherhood consoles us for all those that nature has given you, no doubt in compensation, and also for those, much more numerous, that you have claimed for yourselves" (Carraud and Balzac, 1935, 213).[16] After the birth of her second child, she wrote: "my self is entirely erased in the existence of this new baby" (219).[17] There is one major problem with Carraud as sole source of inspiration, however: she states in a letter to Balzac of November 25, 1835, that she was unable to breast-feed her children. "Too incomplete to have been able to nurse my children myself, I take them straight from their wet nurse's arms, and then they belong to me" (256).[18] We can safely conclude then that the information Balzac sought from Carraud could not have included first-hand knowledge of the pleasurable sensations of breast-feeding.

Although Balzac could have obtained such information from his sister, or even read it in contemporary medical texts, I argue that he may have created Renée's maternal pleasure based at least in part on his own unconscious identification with the male infant. The idea of Balzac identifying with the infant brings to mind the young protagonist Félix's first encounter with Henriette in Balzac's partially autobiographical novel *The Lily of the Valley*, when Félix, whose life experiences often mirror those of Balzac himself, ecstatically says: "I buried my face in that back as a baby hides in its mother's breast, and I kissed those shoulders all over, rubbing my cheek against them" (Balzac, 1898, 19).[19]

In *Memoirs of Two Young Married Women*, Balzac tells the same story of mother infant bliss from the mother's point of view. However, the mother and son are not alone in their pleasure; Renée compares her son to a lover: "there are no caresses of any lover that can equal that of the little rosy fingers" (Balzac, 1894, 192).[20] She then describes the emotional reaction of her habitually cold and distant elderly father-in-law as he watches her nursing his grandson: "The old grandfather is like a child himself; he looks at me admiringly. The first time I went down to breakfast and he saw me eating, and then giving suck to his grandson, he wept. The tears in his dry old eyes, where money usually shines, did me inexpressible good; it seemed to me that the good man felt my joys" (195).[21] Renée completes the portrait of domestic felicity by describing her affection for her husband Louis, "who has first made known to her these wondrous joys […] and taught her the great art of motherhood" (196).[22] Thus, the male spectator, source of maternal joys, is drawn into the circle of maternal desire and legitimates the mother's pleasure within the patriarchal framework of procreation.

As Rollet noted, we must wait almost fifty years for the next example of eroticism in maternal breast-feeding, with Émile Zola's novel *Fécondité*.[23] Published serially in the journal *Aurora* in 1899, the novel seems at first glance to be one long piece of natalist propaganda, with its adoration of the procreating female body and its reiteration of the eighteenth-century cult of the maternal. When Matthieu contemplates his pregnant wife Marianne, he sees her (more specifically her swollen belly) as a sacred object, not a sexual one. The narrator describes Matthieu's emotions in the following terms: "It was higher and truer than the cult of the virgin, the cult of the mother, the glorified and beloved mother, painful and grand, in the passion from which she suffers, for the eternal blossoming of life" (Zola, n.d., 181).[24] This adoration represents the traditional treatment of motherhood, both in literature and in Western culture, which is illustrated here by a comparison both to the Virgin Mary and to the suffering of Jesus Christ, whose self-abnegation for the greater good mothers are expected to imitate. Add to this traditional representation the symbolic resonance of Marianne's name, which exhorts all good Republican women to nurse their own children, as Marianne was the name given to the allegory of the French Republic during the Revolution.[25]

When a young couple comes to visit Marianne after the birth of one of her sons and Matthieu asks them when they plan to have children themselves, the young man refuses to even consider the idea, saying: "You know that, during the nine months of pregnancy and fifteen months of breast-feeding, we won't even be able to kiss each other. That's two years without the slightest caress... Isn't it true, my dear friend, that a reasonable husband, who cares about the good health of mother and child, does not touch his wife during that whole time?" (324).[26] Matthieu replies: "That is a little exaggerated. But there is some truth in it all the same. It is best, in fact, to abstain," advice which follows the medical beliefs of the time. The young husband exclaims: "Abstain, do you hear that, Claire? Huh! What an ugly word. Is that what you want?" (325).[27]

This novel appeared to offer a simple, if eloquent, repetition of the clear division between female sexuality and maternity promoted by Rousseau, which pressured women into pregnancy, nursing, and childcare and into sacrificing their sexuality for the good of the nation and of mankind. This interpretation would support Rollet's claim that breast-feeding became more of a duty than a pleasure by the end of the century (2001, 32). Although these elements certainly dominate Zola's novel, an undercurrent flows just beneath the surface of the text, a small but steady stream of maternal pleasure that reminds us of Balzac's Renée and occasionally inspires the actions of both Matthieu and Marianne. Several scenes showing Marianne nursing the infant Gervais seem fraught with sexual innuendo, hinting of pleasure for the mother, for the (male) infant, and even for the father looking on. In one scene, Marianne suckles Gervais in bed as Matthieu looks on, uniting with the narrator in his lyrical admiration of Marianne's maternal glory:

> [S]he took out of her camisole one of her small hard warrior's breasts, swollen with milk now, blooming like a great flower of life, white and pink; whereas the baby, who could not see well yet, felt around with his hands, reached out with his lips. When he found it, he suckled violently, drinking all of the mother, even including the best of her blood. [...] He [Matthieu] came back, he forgot everything in the rapture of the spectacle. [...] There was no blossoming more glorious, no more sacred symbol of

living eternity: the child at his mother's breast. It was continual childbirth, the mother continued to give all of herself for many long months, finished creating man, opened the fountain of life that flowed onto the world from her flesh. She took the naked, fragile child from her entrails only to take him up against her warm bosom, new refuge of love, where he warmed himself, where he drew nourishment. (Zola, n.d., 320–22)[28]

In a similar scene, the narrator describes the symbiotic union of the mother–infant couple:

She had lowered her beautiful loving eyes on the little one, she watched him suckling eagerly, with a look of immense love, happy even when he hurt her at times, thrilled when he would drink from her too strongly, as she put it. And she continued in a dreamy voice: "My child, belong to another! Oh no, never, never! I would be too jealous, I want him to be made only from me, issued from me, completed by me. He would no longer be my child, if another woman completed him. [...] Dear, dear child! When he suckles so hard, I feel as though my whole being merges with him, it's a delight. (Zola, n.d., 326–27)[29]

After this description of the "delight" ("*délice*" in French) of breast-feeding her son, a word also used too by Balzac's Renée that also has a connotation of intense physical pleasure, Marianne looks up and sees her husband Matthieu, looking at them "very moved," and says: "You're part of it too!" ("Tu en es aussi, toi!") (327). Such a declaration pulls him into the sexually charged space of mother and child and includes him in their physical pleasure. Maternal jouissance seems to exist primarily for the pleasure of the spectator, Matthieu, and by extension all male spectators, who focus their gaze on the mother's exposed breast, lyrically described as "a white breast, soft as silk, whose milk swelled the pink nipple, like a bud from which the flower of life would blossom. [...] the child, on her open and free bosom, suckled in great gulps the warm milk, just as the innumerable greenery drank life from the earth" (342).[30] Marianne exposes her lactating breast again and again throughout the novel, which never fails to arouse both her husband and, it would seem, the narrator as well.

Later, as Matthieu contemplates all the wasted lives in the world due to the lack of mothers nursing their children, he suddenly feels his blood stir at the mere thought of his wife Marianne nursing their son: "A rush of blood warmed Matthieu's heart, as, suddenly, he thought of Marianne, healthy and strong, who would be waiting for him, on the Yeuse bridge, in the vast countryside, with their little Gervais at her breast" (377).[31]

In *Eros and Woman in Zola*, Chantal Bertrand-Jennings saw fertility in this novel as a new morality represented by the maternal figure, "who is thereby cleansed of the original sin of sexuality [...] therefore [...] woman can only truly be accepted as a mother sanctified by her child" (1977, 93).[32] If we may return to Kristeva's concept of maternal jouissance, although the traditional definition of female sexuality focused on sexual intercourse may be denied to the maternal figure in Balzac and Zola, both she and the male spectator managed to find an alternative source of gratification in the experience and the fantasy of breast-feeding. As Kristeva argued: "The loving mother, different from the caring and clinging mother, is someone who has [...] an Other with relation to whom the child will serve as go-between. She will love her child with respect to that Other, and it is through a discourse aimed at that Third Party that the child will be set up as 'loved' for the mother" (1986, 251). Both the orgasmic pleasure of Renée nursing her son and the spectacle of Marianne offering her breast to her twelve children (and, by extension, to the French nation) were intended for the eyes of a third party: whether it be the husband–lover, the male author, or even the reader who participates in the mothers' pleasure, the mediation of the male gaze legitimized maternal jouissance insofar as it encouraged women to fulfill their conjugal and national duty of raising strong and happy young citizens.

In *The Unveiled Breast*, Dominique Gros discusses the complexity of cultural representations of the breast and the insistence on seeing the breast as either sexual or maternal. "[I]n our societies, the male psyche is incapable of conceiving the fact of the female, and especially the lactating female, as a specific and irreducible reality. [...] The ambiguity comes most often from the male gaze. Woman, as for her, knows from experience that her breasts can be for her child or for her partner in turn" (1987, 112). This same ambiguity appeared in nineteenth-century medical and literary discourse as well as in psychoanalytic theory: sensual breast-feeding was tolerated by patriarchal culture so long as it remained subjugated by the gaze of the male Other. When maternal jouissance transgressed the boundaries of patriarchal control, then it became "mastomania," the vice described by Doctor Witkowski in 1898, indulged in only by "hysterical nursing women" (1898, 67). Still seen by contemporary Western culture as primarily sexual, the maternal breast continues to be a focal point for both male fantasies and male anxieties regarding the hidden undercurrents of maternal sexuality.

Wet Nurses and the Corruption of Breast Milk in Hepp and Zola

In late nineteenth-century France, despite high infant mortality rates and innumerable treatises by moralists and medical experts on the evils of mercenary breast-feeding, the wet-nursing industry remained alive and well. In his 1891 novel, *Another's Milk* (*Le Lait d'une autre*), prominent journalist and naturalist Alexandre Hepp told a disturbing story of a male child utterly corrupted by the moral depravity of an ignorant wet nurse. As Zola would do eight years later in *Fécondité*, Hepp attempted to use the persuasive power of fiction to convince parents of the dangers inherent in hiring a wet nurse. Although the ostensible message of the author in favor of maternal breast-feeding and against wet-nursing seems clear, the unequivocally negative portrayal of breast milk as a destructive force in *Another's Milk* reveals a fear of feminine sexuality that even the sanctity of motherhood cannot erase.

Hepp's novel, while particularly graphic, followed a long tradition of publications by French moralists and intellectuals condemning wet nurses and their industry. The title of one chapter of Angélique Le Rebours' breast-feeding handbook for mothers unambiguously stated her firm belief that "the practice of putting children out to nurse is a cause of depopulation" (1798, 33).[33] In addition to the high mortality rate, Le Rebours takes issue specifically with the concept of the precious infant being entrusted to an ignorant stranger, a concern often cited by previous treatises going back to sixteenth-century royal surgeon Ambroise Paré, who wrote in 1573 that "the morals and vices of the wet nurse flow into children almost with their milk" (Paré, 1840, II: 686).[34] Le Rebours condemned wet-nursing even more strongly:

> What strange abuse is it then to pervert this natural nobility of men that comes to us from nature, to corrupt body and mind […]

by having the child take the degenerate nourishment of a foreign
and bastardized milk? (Le Rebours, 1798, 66–67)[35]

Traditional arguments in favor of maternal nursing, such as the
loss of the child's affections to a stranger, the moral imperative of
conforming to the "natural" order, and the dangers of maternal illness
from suppressed milk, appeared again and again in hundreds of printed
works throughout the eighteenth and nineteenth centuries, including
dozens of medical theses. Among the many dangers of hiring a wet
nurse, authorities often cited a lack of moral character – a serious health
issue at a time when sexual activity was believed to corrupt a woman's
milk. Fanny Fay-Sallois, in her history of the wet-nursing industry,
summarizes the belief of nineteenth-century doctors as to the effects
of sexual activity on breast milk: "They fear the possible consequences:
the immediate one is the alteration of the milk" (1980, 229).[36] A breast-
feeding manual from 1834, *Manuel des nourrices*, stated that "orgasm alters
the nature of the milk, deprives it of its sweetness and thus causes serious
illness in the nursling" (Bayle-Mouillard, 1834, 53).[37] An anonymous
pamphlet published in 1851, "Wet Nurses Unmasked!", denounced the
deadly effects of "a corrupted milk suckled from a wet nurse" on the
thousands of Parisian infants, or *petits Paris*, shipped out to the country
each year (*Les Nourrices démasquées!*, 1851, 17).[38] But judging from
statistics gathered by George Sussman, Fanny Fay-Sallois, and others,
these repetitive tirades had little or no effect on actual practices. By the
account of the director of a wet nurses' bureau in 1875, 20,000 Parisian
babies per year were being sent out to wet nurses (Vacher, 1873, 5).

Increasing fears of the depopulation of the French nation after
France's defeat by the Prussians in 1870 intensified the pressure on
mothers to nurse their own children. In his 1897 treatise on depopulation, Dr Jacques Bertillon wrote: "All the departments, without
exception, present a decrease in the birth rate since the beginning of
the century" (1897, 9).[39] In 1875, Jean-Baptiste Desplace wrote that
despite more than thirty years of warnings about the risks of depopulation, "we persist in our guilty indifference and in our infanticidal
habits. As in the past, the population of our cities sends its children out
to wet nurses, who in turn remain attached to their routines. Nurslings
continue to die" (1875, 10–11).[40]

As the anti-wet-nursing rhetoric grew more heated, negative
representations of wet nurses in literature and popular culture became

more prevalent. In 1896, Zola penned an article for *Le Figaro* on depopulation in which he cited his long-standing intention to write a novel on the subject, provisionally entitled *Waste* (*Le Déchet*). This project would become the novel *Fécondité* (1899), in which Zola systematically laid out all his carefully accumulated demographic and sociological data on the crisis of the French family. The *Bulletin of the National Alliance for the Increase of the French Population*, an organization founded by Dr. Jacques Bertillon in 1896, and of which Zola was a founding member, highlighted the realistic accuracy of Zola's novel: "The author seems to us to have simply (this is the mark of genius) written what we all have right in front of us at every moment" (*Bulletin*, 1899, 47).[41] In an interview on maternal breast-feeding in the feminist newspaper *La Fronde* (*Revolt*), in 1899, Zola stated unequivocally that in his opinion, hiring a wet nurse was "an appalling tactic that inevitably brings trouble. A child nursed by a stranger draws his life force from a new element and can absorb its vices and its maladies" (Lefébure, 1899, 1).[42] Not surprisingly, Dr. Boutan, Zola's medical spokesperson in *Fécondité*, echoes these sentiments: "merely the choice to engage in this profession of wet-nursing puts them, for me, at the bottom of the human ladder. There is no more revolting or degrading industry" (Zola, n.d., 394).[43]

Unlike Zola's original project, which would have described society's problems around procreation without proposing a solution, *Fécondité* offers a utopic vision of the ideal French family represented by protagonists Mathieu and Marianne Froment and their abundant offspring. In comparison with the many negative examples in the novel, including wet nurses, bad mothers, *meneuses* (women whose job it was to take infants to their wet nurses' homes in the country), and couples who use contraception, Zola's lyrical tributes to Marianne provide a positive model for responsible, natural motherhood. Through this utopic family, breast milk becomes the catalyst for world peace and harmony as it flows through the heroine:

Marianne [...] was not the only one feeding her young; the April sap swelled the plowed fields, made the woods quiver, and raised up the tall grasses where it was drowning. And, beneath her, from the earth's bosom in a continuous birth, she could feel this tidal wave that reached her, filled her, renewed her milk, as the milk was streaming from her breast. And it was the flood of milk flowing through the earth, the flood of eternal life for the eternal harvest of beings. (Zola, n.d., 346)[44]

Marianne's flowing milk becomes a force for good, feeding the nation in much the same way as the plentiful grains that surround her. This image echoes revolutionary rhetoric on breast-feeding and Republican virtues of a century earlier, exemplified by the speech given by Hérault de Séchelles, president of the National Convention, in front of the Fountain of Regeneration.[45]

Feminist critics have analyzed the role of breast milk in *Fécondité*. Chantal Bertrand-Jennings describes "good" motherhood, which includes breast-feeding, as the only way for women in Zola's novels to be deemed morally suitable: "motherhood becomes the redemption of sexual sin, that only a woman considered a good mother can be accepted, whereas other women are presented as either negative characters or *femmes fatales*" (1977, 97).[46] Catherine Malinas's analysis of "the cult of the breast" in *Fécondité* builds on Bertrand-Jennings's conclusion, stating that "in the blossoming of the woman after motherhood, Zola only distinguishes the breast, this breast whose sustaining function justifies in his eyes its erotic function" (Malinas, 1986, 175).[47] For these critics, Marianne's joyous procreation, her abundant milk production, and her abstention from sex while breast-feeding all represent the author's efforts to sanctify feminine sexuality through its regulation within the patriarchal institution of motherhood. When safely contained within the boundaries of virtuous motherhood, breast milk can be seen as an unambiguously positive life-giving force essential to the survival of the French nation.

An earlier novel that may have inspired Zola offers a much darker view of the wet-nursing industry as well as breast-feeding in general. Eight years before the publication of *Fécondité*, noted journalist, colleague, and disciple of Zola, Alexandre Hepp, published *Another's Milk*, a novel intended to expose the evils of wet-nursing. Hepp clearly had a predilection for scandalous topics, as evidenced by his 1885 novel *The Worn Out Man* (*L'Épuisé*), the story of a man with a decadent past who passes his moral defects in the form of hereditary syphilis down to his deformed and monstrous son. Its publication in the newspaper *Le Matin* was suspended because readers found it "too risqué" (Simond, 1901, 314) and full of details one reviewer described as "nauseating and smutty, more appropriate to medical literature than to a novel (Boissin,

1888, 195).[48] Perhaps due to this plethora of titillating details, *L'Épuisé* seems to have sold well, being in its twentieth edition by the time Hepp published *Another's Milk* in 1891. Hepp's penchant for salacious subjects may have contributed to the popular and critical success of *Another's Milk*; its publication was hailed by glowing reviews. *The Literary Year* (*L'année littéraire*) praised the novel for its "terrible tableaus, painted with a rare vigor by a writer whose thinking is exceptionally sound, under its audacity" ("Compte rendu du *Lait d'une autre*," 1891, 199).[49] Lucien Muhlfeld wrote in *The White Journal* (*La Revue blanche*):

> His novel, with a largely intelligible symbolism [...] will convince [young mothers] of the superiority of maternal breast-feeding over wet-nursing and all the more over bottle-feeding. Mr. Hepp will do enormous harm to the wet-nursing bureaus; and who will blame him? (Muhlfeld, 1891, 78)[50]

Hepp's novel attracted the attention not only of literary critics, but also of medical authorities. In an article published in the *Gazette of Gynecology*, in 1898, Dr Léon Petit ranted:

> Good wet nurse! Ah! Ah! Good wet nurse! Those are three words that should never be put together! [...] But do you even know her, this woman to whom you are going to entrust your child? Are you forgetting that the morals of this stranger will have a constant influence on this yet unformed mind, an influence that can alter an entire life? (Petit, 1898, 116)[51]

Later in the same article, Dr Petit recommends *Another's Milk*, which he calls "the painfully true story of a child odiously sullied by one of these wenches" (117).[52] By treating Hepp's novel as truth rather than fiction and citing it as evidence in a medical journal, Petit legitimizes the moralistic message of Hepp's novel in an era of pronatalist propaganda based on fears of depopulation. By 1899, the year of the publication of Zola's *Fécondité*, Hepp's novel was in its nineteenth edition (Hepp, 1898–99, n.p.).

Despite these signs of literary success, Zolian criticism to date seems to have overlooked the possibility of Hepp's novel having influenced Zola. In his comprehensive summary of scholarship on *Fécondité*, David Baguley mentions Eugène Brieux's plays as having repeated the themes of *Fécondité* but neglects to mention Hepp at all, despite a very public dispute between Hepp and Brieux in 1901 on the question of intellectual property and the subject of wet-nursing (1973, 171–72).[53] During the incident with Brieux, Hepp claimed that *Another's Milk* had been "serialized in numerous periodicals" and that it was "not at all unknown to the public" (Hauser, 1901).[54] Zola and Hepp were certainly acquainted with each other, at least professionally; both men wrote for the periodical *Le Voltaire* in the 1880s, where Hepp replaced Zola as theatre critic and eventually became editor-in-chief (Dumesnil, 1945, 248). Zola wrote Hepp a letter on November 5, 1882, praising another of his novels, *L'Ami de Madame Alice*, which had just come out (Zola, 1983–2010, vol. 4, p. 339). I also found a first edition of Zola's novel *La Débâcle* from 1892, the year after the publication of *Another's Milk*, autographed by the author to "Alexandre Hepp, son dévoué confrère" (Walwyn-Jones, 2013). From all this, I have concluded that it is likely that Zola would have been familiar with Hepp's novel on the dangers of wet-nursing before he composed *Fécondité*.

In his preface, Hepp states his hope that mothers will read his novel "with terror" (1891, ii) and will think twice about abandoning their children to the care of a complete stranger. The subtitle of the novel clarifies even further the intended message: *Novel on the Dangers of Mercenary Breast-Feeding* (*Roman sur les dangers de l'allaitement mercenaire*). Hepp claims that the novel is based on the true story of a man he has met, saying: "I respect, admire and pity him" (ii).[55] The premise seems to fulfill its author's intent: the Baron Michel Cavin's wife, Geneviève, on the advice of both her mother and her doctor, refuses to breast-feed their newborn son Maurice. Instead, she chooses a wet nurse, an unwed mother from the village of Sennelisse, named, like Zola's protagonist, Marianne, after the symbol of the French republic.

Despite her name and its connotations of virtuous Republican motherhood, Marianne's depravity becomes apparent from the moment she enters the story; she spends the last night before her departure for Paris having sex with every available male in the village. The narrator makes no mystery of her promiscuity, even adding an ironic aside about the effort expended by the village men: "[S]he finished her rounds; they took her even in front of the cemetery; they must be exhausted!" (50).[56] Just before dawn, Marianne comes across old Gérard, the elderly baker who owns most of the village, opening his bakery on the main village square. He is described as having "a square and hairless chin, eyes without pity, deeply set under surly white eyebrows" (50–51).[57] The young woman decides to offer herself to him out of idle curiosity.

> Slowly she comes and smiles at him, very fresh. And curiosity piques her, a need to know, to discover what is left of him, that one! Young men, an old man! And she comes closer, passively, with an evil idea of being good, and the old man wraps her in his arms, he kneads her, grinds against her; then he looks at himself, for a second he waits, he has wild hopes for his dead being. Oh! A moment of horrible torture makes his face go pale. Nothing. And yet he still feels desire, a desire that grips, devastates the trembling old man's face. And the girl bursts out laughing. (Hepp, 1891, 51–52)[58]

But when she starts to leave, he sits on a nearby ledge and gestures for her to join him. She does so willingly, "delighting in giving him some pleasure" (52).[59] The reader wonders what is coming, and considering the fairly explicit nature of the previous paragraph, it seems anything is possible. But old Gérard's chosen alternative to satisfying his lingering sexual desire turns out to be the act of nursing from Marianne's breast, there in the main square.

> Then, with his claws, he opens her pink jacket that loosely covers her flesh, reaches down into her large rough blouse, the wool drawstring of which was hanging loose. And for a long time his old man's fingers explore, his lips drool over the magnificence of this bosom, and he outlines and licks her swollen breasts clean with his tongue. And the girl says: "Suckle, old man, just to see!" Then the old man coaxes the nipple into his withered mouth, moves his hard and toothless jaws, and takes in a fountain of pure milk. (Hepp, 1891, 52–53)[60]

After letting him drink, she pulls back, exclaiming: "Enough, that hurts! He would drink it all up!" And leaving Gérard, "bent over, all smeared with white, sucking on his lips: and as he tries to find her again, she has already fled, taking with her his saliva and the bruises of the old man's bites" (53).[61] Later, when the Parisian who has hired her to nurse his son notices the bruises, the wet nurse tearfully confesses to having nursed her own baby one last time before she left the village, even though she knew she shouldn't have because her milk was already the legal property of her new employer (67).

Let us examine the vocabulary used to describe this scene. Hepp's narrator chooses negatively connoted words to describe the old man. First, the description of Gérard's "hairless chin" "and his 'eyes without pity' paints an unsympathetic and unattractive picture. Words emphasizing his advanced age, like "surly white eyebrows," "his old man's fingers," "his hardened toothless jaws," and "his withered mouth" effectively contrast with the erotic description of the engorged breasts ("the magnificence of this bosom ... the swollen breasts").

Instead of portraying the wet nurse as an animal, this scene seems to juxtapose the animalistic, almost violent sexual desire of the old man ("his claws," "he kneads her, crushes her") to the youth of the wet nurse ("very fresh") and the purity of her milk ("a fountain of pure milk"). Her pride in her milk ("it's beautiful, isn't it? she exclaimed with pride") seems to contradict the prevailing medical theories of the time that claimed a woman's low moral character would corrupt her milk. Whether her milk itself is pure or not, the narrator clearly marks her misuse of it as impure in the scene with old Gérard. When she pulls away, she leaves Gérard "tout barbouillé de blanc" ("all smeared in white"). The *Robert Dictionary* defines the verb "barbouiller" as both a familiar and pejorative expression meaning "to cover in a dirty substance." The use of the word "barbouiller" also infantilizes the old man, since it is most often said of children; the references to his lack of teeth and his constant drooling also mark his similarities to a nursling. However, the same characteristics that might be acceptable in an infant (drooling, toothlessness, avidity to nurse) become revolting in an old man.

Even more intriguing than the detailed physical description of the act is its placement in the sexual economy of the novel. When Marianne has sex with the entire male population of Sennelisse, each of those acts, while clearly marked as immoral by the narrator, merits only a few lines of description. In contrast, the scene of old Gérard breast-feeding with clear sexual intent in the village square gains prominence in the narrative not only by its length (about three pages in the original edition), but also by its placement; it represents Marianne's final hurrah before she boards the coach for her new life in Paris. The acts of sexual intercourse and that of breast-feeding the old man seem to blend together in the novel as two ways of demonstrating the depraved nature of the main character.

Most revealing is the way in which the village gossip frames the incident of the old man breast-feeding as a failed economic exchange:

"[A]h, he didn't waste any time, old Gérard, getting the breast and the milk for nothing! That's worth good money, in the City she'll get paid for that" (54).[62] The implied comparison of wet nurses to prostitutes, selling their bodies for money, completes the transformation of the maternal breast into an object of male desire that can be bought and sold. It also provides a moral condemnation of the wet-nursing industry, implying that the very act of selling her milk to strangers corrupts and perverts Marianne, and, by extension, all wet nurses.

The contrast between the old man and the attractive young woman would certainly have reminded nineteenth-century readers of the image of "Roman Charity," popular in the visual arts. The author's emphasis on the sexualized breast-feeding scene both horrifies and fascinates the reader in much the same way that portrayals of the theme of Roman Charity, with their self-proclaimed uplifting message and their underlying eroticism, fascinated spectators in the *salons*. Valerius Maximus, in approximately 30 CE, first tells a contemporary story of a young woman who nursed her mother in prison to save her life. He then compares this Roman tale to the foreign (presumably Greek) legend of Pero and Cimon, on which most subsequent artistic representations were based. After Cimon was imprisoned and left to starve, writes Valerius, "A man in extreme old age, she put him like a baby to her breast and fed him. Men's eyes are riveted in amazement when they see the painting of this act and renew the features of the long bygone incident in astonishment at the spectacle now before them, believing that in those silent outlines of limbs they see living and breathing bodies" (2000, 501–2). The element of spectacle is a key part of the picture even in Valerius' account; the daughter's piety is constructed and reanimated by the male spectator's gaze. While the Roman story generally glorified the nursing couple as a dignified representation of filial piety, the imagery was later incorporated into Christian iconography as representing two of the Seven Acts of Mercy: feeding the hungry and visiting those in prison (*L'allégorie dans la peinture*, 1986, 38–39).

Despite the Roman version featuring a mother and daughter couple, the old man nursed by a beautiful young daughter has been the preferred theme of the majority of artists from Pompeii onward. Art historian Adolf de Ceuleneer has explained this choice as follows: "It is not that they were unaware of the story of the Roman woman; but they would have been convinced, and rightly so, that from an artistic point of view [...] for the psychological effect produced, an old man nursed by his daughter was more suitable" (1919, 196).[63] In the catalogue of a 1986 exhibit on Roman Charity in art, Alain Mérot takes this a step further, posing the following question: "Was the great popularity of the theme, until the nineteenth century, due to the its rich emotional content and its incestuous nature?" (1986, 16).[64] Robert Rosenblum speculated that the paternal version remained dominant because it could "veil an erotic motif under the pall of a dungeon and the light of daughterly virtue" (1972, 49).

Jean Goujon's bas relief showing the resurgence of the motif during the French Renaissance might have been familiar to Parisians in the nineteenth century, since it was on view in the exterior Square Courtyard (*Cour Carrée*) of the Louvre until 1807 and subsequently displayed in a courtyard of the French national school of the fine arts, the École des Beaux-Arts ("Provenance de l'œuvre de Jean Goujon," 2012). Rubens painted four different versions of the scene; Greuze's version was part of private collections in France until the 1830s. There were two paintings on the theme in the 1765 Salon; in his Salon critique, philosopher Denis Diderot described in great detail his own imagined version, in which the woman would have "good, fat and large breasts, very full of milk"[65] (1765, unpag.).

A scene in a best-selling 1777 novel by Marmontel called *The Incas* described explorer Las Casas being nursed back to health by a beautiful young Indian woman. In the scene's description, the woman describes herself as Las Casas's surrogate daughter:

> What are you afraid of, man of peace and of sweetness? Am I not your daughter? Are you not our father? My beloved has told me that so many times! He would give his blood for you. As for me, I am offering you my milk. Deign to draw life from this breast that you have caused to quiver so many times, when I heard about the prodigies of your goodness. (Marmontel, 1991, 165)[66]

The novel inspired Louis Hersent's painting "Las Casas Cured by Savages," first exhibited in the official Salon of 1808 and then again in 1814 and 1824 (now in a private collection in the USA) (Sperling, 2011, 47–71). Hersent's painting was also reproduced in an engraving by Pierre Michel Adam in 1823 (Davis, 2006, 117). Marie-Hélène Gachet, in a 1985 article on Roman Charity, reported finding more than 200 examples of art works featuring this motif, including many engravings that made the images available to a more general public (1984, 85).

Alain Mérot wrote of the legend of Roman Charity: "It is obscure in its intentions and unclear in its message. The rapture it evokes is perverse" (1986, 16).[67] The sexual depiction of breast-feeding in Hepp's novel, while not at all obscure in its intentions, evokes a similar perverse rapture in the reader. Hepp subverts the mother–child couple, replacing the innocent child with an impotent, toothless, sexually depraved old man, and the self-sacrificing mother with a wanton wet nurse who sells her body for money. By converting an image generally associated with filial piety and Catholic mercy into an erotic scene totally deprived of all moral or even practical value (since the old man is not in need of sustenance), Hepp uses the perverse fascination of the reader to enhance his condemnation of the immoral wet nurse. In giving her milk first to old Gérard and then to a Parisian infant, Marianne functions as a negative example for the young mothers to whom Hepp dedicates the novel. But given the voyeuristic pleasures of the erotic passages in the novel, it seems likely that men were Hepp's intended readers.

Upon her arrival in the Cavin household in Paris, Marianne becomes little Maurice's primary caregiver and cherishes the special bond with her nursling to an unhealthy degree. The vocabulary the narrator uses to describe their relationship is charged with sexual tension, with connotations of possession and masochistic pleasure:

> She loved to hear him scream, like he used to, for her to take possession of him once more, to calm him by herself, with her milk! Then when she showed him dozing, as if by a miracle, on her breast, she would thank him for staying faithful to her, for loving her milk above all. (Hepp, 1891, 126)[68]

From the start, her milk corrupts the innocent child: "The instinct drunk with the other's milk was doing its work. The cursed milk of the stranger was embedding itself in his flesh" (186).[69] Despite her initial efforts to resist temptation, the wet nurse will molest the young toddler shortly after weaning him, touching and kissing him in explicitly inappropriate ways. When the child's father finally realizes the truth, it is too late to save his son from complete moral ruin. The pernicious influence of the wet nurse is irreversible: "the venom of her milk prospers [...] the work of his destruction is definitive and predestined" (324).[70] The message seems clear: children (particularly male children) entrusted to the care of lower-class, morally depraved, and sexually avid women will suffer dire and ruinous consequences from maternal neglect, even if the wet nurse is under the supervision of the parents in their own home.

While most proponents of maternal breast-feeding of the time (including, for the most part, Zola) chose to highlight other aspects of wet-nursing, such as the ignorance or poor hygiene of the wet nurse or even the dire consequences of wet-nursing for the nurse's own child, Hepp focuses on sexual depravity as the primary evil. Hepp's sexualization of the breast-feeding relationship, while shocking even today, was far from new in the nineteenth century. Prior to the Enlightenment, as we saw in Chapter 1, sexual pleasure while breast-feeding was touted by medical authorities such as Laurent Joubert as nature's way of enticing women to nurse. As we have seen, when the Enlightenment's definition of motherhood carefully segregated the maternal and the sexual, the idea of pleasurable nursing could no longer be used as legitimate enticement (Lastinger, 1996). Sexual pleasure in the nursing relationship, at least in literary and medical discourse, thus became the territory of the evil wet nurse as well as evidence of moral dissolution, as illustrated by Hepp's novel.

Unlike many of Zola's wet nurses, Marianne in Hepp's novel is passionately devoted to her charge, keeps herself and the child clean and well-fed, does not drink to excess, and does everything in her power to protect and nurture little Maurice. When her own child dies back in the village, his death is accorded little more than a footnote; we're told she had never even asked about him (1891, 174). The primary danger she poses to little Maurice, then, is not physical, but moral; with her milk comes the contamination of vice.

Soon after her arrival, Michel catches the wet nurse extracting milk from the crying infant's nipples. The nurse's nonchalant reaction ("Oh, sir, you don't know about that! All babies have milk, they come with it at birth and you have to get rid of it!" [81])[71] does nothing to relieve the father's horror at the spectacle, and the nurse's attentions to the infant are described in terms that are both violent and vaguely sensual. "The wet nurse kneaded him, working his nipples" (81).[72] In his guilt, Michel connects his son's suffering to that of his wife when her milk came in:

> the mother had just had a brush with death because she stubbornly
> chose to sterilize that sacred milk! And now, the innocent babe

was suffering in turn, and this is what would have caused him his
first pain? Geneviève, the child, affected by the same cause? Oh!
That was too much, and the child's moan as his mother's milk
was removed from him […] reverberated loudly within Michel.
(Hepp, 1891, 81–82)[73]

The scene foretells the sexual initiation to come, with the verb
"triturer" (to knead or manipulate compulsively) and its sexual
connotation in particular, drawing a link of perversion between the
mother, the nurse, and the infant that will eventually lead to the boy's
destruction.

The beginning of the child's molestation appears almost as a natural
extension of the sexualized nursing relationship.

[T]he little one's so-white body, with its firm and chubby lines,
became slowly visible in the darkness. It emerged, it stretched
out brazenly, and it tempted her. […] She presented her breast
again to the little weaned child, he took it, he recognized it,
he rediscovered it with joy and he went to sleep. […] And
the pleasure for her was all the more vibrant because she had
postponed it; now, the child received this violent affection on a
regular basis, and the girl from Sennelisse justified it in her own
eyes, saying to herself that it came from her heart. (Hepp, 1891,
156; 158; 165)[74]

The wet nurse, cut off from normal sexual relations by her social
situation as a live-in domestic servant, and deprived of the sexual
satisfaction of nursing after the child is weaned, seeks gratification in
the only form available to her: through sexual contact with the weaned
child. As a result, she is demonized by the narrator, who compares her
milk to venom and denounces it as "cursed milk."

The negative connotations of the working-class wet nurse's milk and
its pernicious influence might be expected in a novel whose message
serves as a condemnation of wet-nursing; interestingly, however,
the milk of the child's aristocratic mother seems equally destructive.
Shortly after Maurice's birth, Geneviève, his frivolous, flighty, and
beautiful young mother, suffers from what some doctors of the time
still called "milk fever" when her milk comes in. The mother's milk,
deprived of its natural purpose of nourishment for the child, appears as
a violent, irrepressible force that endangers the mother's life as well as

her sanity. Her husband Michel, the only sympathetic character in the novel, is drawn into the battle as well.

> Then, bent over, terrified, Michel uncovered her breasts. The sheets flew, and Michel received a splash of milk right in the face. It was an enormous rocket, a furious gushing from two painful, formidable, white, vein-covered breasts. And those veins seemed to crack, to writhe, and to crawl over the swelling globes like snakes. And sometimes too it looked like the unleashing of a storm on her bosom; it oscillated under the formation, the momentum of a gusher that was welling up; then when everything had let go, with powerful jerking movements, it kept flowing, flowed on forever, spread out, liquid, fluid, without end, everywhere, all over her, and all over the bed. "The milk!" cried Geneviève. "It's coming, it's coming, it's coming!" And under the streaming liquid that was coming out of her, flooding her, with occasional impetuous waterspouts, she was fainting, rolling, losing her soul. (Hepp, 1891, 74–75)[75]

Michel, the father, his face covered in milk, reminds the reader of old Gérard, "all smeared in white." In Michel's case, however, the scene is not overtly sexual but rather menacing and brutal; "an enormous rocket," almost an assault, replete with connotations of the loss of maternal paradise ("like snakes") and God's punishment in the form of violent weather ("storm," "waterspout").

The waste of life-giving milk and its forceful involuntary expulsion from Geneviève's convulsing body invite a comparison with the late nineteenth-century medical establishment's obsession with masturbation and its waste of valuable sperm, echoed by Zola's narrator in *Fécondité*: "the flow of semen turned away from its true purpose, fallen on the pavement where nothing would grow..." (Zola, n.d., 109–10).[76] In his seminal text, *Onanism*, first published in Latin in 1760 and widely distributed in French in 1764, Samuel Tissot warned of the dire consequences of masturbation for the male body (Foucault, 2001, 163 n. 6). Medical morality tales on masturbation, such as Paul Bonnetain's *Charlot Is Having Fun* (*Charlot s'amuse*, 1884), were common in the late 1800s and garnered considerable attention from the press (Przybos, 2005). As Julia Przybos notes in her study of Bonnetain's work: "Between 1760 and 1925, a dozen volumes of medical vulgarization have been found in which masturbation is featured among the major preoccupations of hygienists" (2005, 174).[77] Preoccupied by fears of depopulation, Émile Zola and other French naturalists denounced "*la fraude*" – a general term referring to the waste of any sperm not emitted in the cause of repopulating France. These same writers made similar arguments regarding mother's milk, the waste of which led not only to high infant mortality rates but also to debilitating physical maladies for the mother. In the words of Zola's medical authority in *Fécondité*, Dr. Boutan: "Just think about it! One cannot trick an organ with impunity. [...] Any function that does not occur in the normal order of things becomes a permanent danger of turmoil" (Zola, n.d., 572).[78] Although Dr. Boutan is referring here to masturbation, he could as easily be talking about the consequences of refusing to breast-feed one's children, as nature intended. In the last few pages of *Fécondité*, the parallel between semen and milk continues in the narrator's elegy to nature: "Always new seeds gave birth to new harvests, the sun always rose from the horizon, milk flowed without end from nourishing bosoms, eternal sap of living humanity" (1031).[79]

Throughout his treatise on onanism, Tissot compares sperm to other bodily fluids, or humors, including milk. For Tissot, milk is "a simply nourishing liquid," as opposed to semen, which is "an active liquid" (1797, 2–3),[80] from which he concludes that excessive emission of sperm does more damage than overproduction of milk. He compares the health risks of men who ejaculate too frequently (the main topic of his book) to those of women who produce too much milk:

> The illnesses that women experience are as easily explained as those of men. The humor that women lose being less precious, less refined than men's sperm, its loss does not weaken them as promptly; but when they lose an excess of milk, their nervous system is weaker, and naturally inclined to spasms, and their illnesses are violent. (Tissot, 1797, 73–74)[81]

While French physicians disputed the theory of humorism as the underlying cause of illnesses as early as the 1810s, the belief in the dangers of *lait répandu*, or spilled milk, remained strong in both medical and popular discourse throughout the nineteenth century, seen as late as 1845 in *A Medical and Philosophical History of Woman*:

> The milk she refuses to give her infant is transformed into a deadly poison, which becomes for her an endless source of pain

and torment [...] The unnatural mothers who liberate themselves from this duty typically pay dearly for this crime against nature. The milk that they have the cruelty to deny to their children is carried indistinctly to all their organs and wreaks the most terrible havoc. We have seen women lose their reason, their hearing, as a result of milk deposits in parts of their brain. (Menville, 1845, 177; quoted in Fay-Sallois, 1980, 125)[82]

Drs. Bayle and Gilbert, in their 1858 *Dictionary of Daily and Domestic Medicine*, called the theory of *le lait répandu*, "a fantasy of the imagination and of ignorance" (1858–59, 131).[83] While Dr. Auguste Debay also refuted the humorist explanation in his *Hygiene and Physiology of Marriage*, which went through 172 editions between 1848 and 1888 (Pryzbos, 2005, 174), his alternative theory of an "excess of life" in the uterus that moves naturally to the lactating breasts after parturition leads to the same result for the mother who refuses to nurse:

The reabsorption of milk is almost always harmful to the organ that secretes it, and has an effect, furthermore, on general health; the most common consequences of this sudden suppression manifests itself in illnesses known by the vulgar name of *lait répandu*, or by swellings, hardenings, abscesses in the parenchyma of the breasts; later, by tumors, ulcers, and sometimes by a horrible illness, cancer! Cancer has no cure. (Debay, 1862, 412–13)[84]

Debay's description of the habitual masturbator, in the same volume, while it does not mention cancer, sounds just as dire, echoing Tissot's lists of symptoms: "they are pale, bloated, lazy, fearful, cowardly, morally and physically debased. [...] Soon he falls into a complete state of debility and life abandons him in turn" (1862, 315; 219).[85]

Another sign of the parallel between the anti-masturbation and the anti-wet-nursing movements can be seen in the late nineteenth-century obsession with spermatorrhoea, described by Elizabeth Stephens as "a fear of male leakiness, of an oozing fluidity" (2008, 209). Stephens compares spermatorrhoea in men to female hysteria, framing both phenomena as medico-psychological manifestations of gender anxiety in late nineteenth-century France. In her words, "the convulsive gesture and rigid body of the female hysteric can be read as phallic, just as the incontinent leakiness of the spermatorrhoeaic body can easily be read as feminized. [...] Spermatorrhoea and hysteria provide cautionary narratives that demonstrate how imperceptibly, but dangerously, pleasure and fertility could be transformed into pain and debilitating disease" (202).

Similarly, Janet Beizer, in her analysis of the definition and treatments of hysteria in nineteenth century France in *Ventriloquized Bodies*, remarks that "doctors repeatedly paint woman as slave to her secretions, unable to control her dripping, flowing, spurting, oozing bodily fluids" (1993, 41). Beizer then recounts the case of a woman suffering from "galactorrhea," or the overproduction of milk, from an 1859 treatise on hysteria by Dr. Pierre Briquet: "At the least movement, the milk would spurt out [of the breast] like out of a watering can [...] Pressure made the milk shoot out in multiple jets, and as soon as the pressure ceased, the milk flows constantly drop by drop, and so the patient collects it with the help of a vase hanging at her belt. When the patient gets up or sits on her bed, drops of milk give way to numerous spurts" (Briquet, 1859, 482–83; quoted in Beizer, 1993, 42).[86] Beizer comments on the male doctor's "undisguised fascination along with a dose of sensationalism" in his description of the woman's spurting breasts, citing this example as evidence of her theory that the definition of hysteria in late nineteenth-century France was shifting from a *uterine* illness to a *maternal* one (37; 42). Ironically, in Bonnetain's cautionary tale on masturbation, Charlot attends a seminar on hysteria where the learned male doctor presents a patient suffering from nymphomania and hysterical fits; horrified, Charlot recognizes his own mother (Bonnetain, 1883, 293–95).

Just as Charlot's mother was possessed by an uncontrollable force of nature that threatened to take her sanity or even her life, in Hepp's novel, Geneviève's unruly female body betrays her. "And while they tried to master, to check this milk that did not want to surrender, Geneviève was emitting sing-song laments, and lying with arched back sideways on the bed, was losing herself more and more in a delirium that frightened everyone" (Hepp, 1891, 76).[87] Geneviève herself, disgusted by the abundance of fluid flowing from her body, compares her milk to her own blood, giving her the illusion of bleeding to death:

And still, inexhaustible, in white and yellow spurts (*flux*), the milk escaped, and it descended all along her sides, slipped, and in places on her belly it stagnated as though in a deep basin. And

> Geneviève had hidden her hands in her terror of getting them wet in all that, in her disgust at the superb abundance that was irrupting from her body. Oh! This milk that refused to stop, it seemed like blood to her, like she was losing it through a thousand cuts, that her life was running out! And in her head all this was dancing around, melting together, and it seemed to her suddenly that in her brain too everything was turning to liquid. (Hepp, 1891, 76–77)[88]

The word "*flux*" ("spurts"), typically used in French to describe the loss of blood, reinforces the idea that Geneviève's endless flow of milk represents a draining of her life force. When the doctor arrives, he expresses his stupefaction at the sheer abundance of milk and even some regret at having talked his patient out of nursing her own child: "But what sap, what riches! No, never had he found himself faced with such a manifestation; milk, milk everywhere! Enough to feed a nursery! What an admirable prodigy! Ah, if only he had known!" (77).[89] As Geneviève's life hangs in the balance, her husband Michel sees her milk as a force for good that has been corrupted by their unnatural, even immoral, actions:

> Yes, she is suffering, yes, everything is put into question, and it is because we are not on the true path. Oh! This alone shows it. We want to escape the duty for which we were created, triumph over nature, and there you go! We deserve it. Oh no, we should not have done this! The milk, her milk that belonged to our son, this milk that we are trying to banish now like a poison, instead of fearing and cursing it, what joy, what security it would have meant for our household! (Hepp, 1891, 78–79)[90]

Instead of the sanctified elixir it was meant to be, like the life-giving sap represented by Marianne's maternal milk in *Fécondité*, Geneviève's milk has become a poison, endangering her health and possibly her life, all because she refused to follow nature's course and breast-feed her child.

While *Another's Milk* and *Fécondité* have many striking similarities, their representation of breast milk mirrors the principal difference between them. With the dedication of his novel, Hepp clearly indicates both the polemic underlying his book and its intended audience: "To the woman who breast-feeds. Mother who will not have an intermediary between your son and you, this book is your triumph and I dedicate it to you!" (1891, n.p.).[91] However, the dutiful mother to whom the novel is dedicated remains absent from Hepp's representation, except in Michel's imagination before their son's birth, as he tries to convince his wife to breast-feed: "Holy, purified, inaccessible, the woman who breast feeds. Her duty cannot be shared. The love that created it, cleanses and withers her; she is withdrawn in her mission, the slavery, of a new virginity…" (1891, 21–22).[92] Ironically, it is the thought of the purity and inaccessibility of the breast-feeding mother that finally convinces Michel to accept the idea of a wet nurse, to preserve his sexual relations with his wife. This selfish, sexually motivated impulse perverts Geneviève's milk, transforming it into a destructive force. Whereas the milk of Zola's heroine Marianne flows serenely through *Fécondité*, symbolizing the life-giving force of an epic French future filled with large happy families, the images of breast milk in Hepp's novel remain, as we have seen, unequivocally menacing and even destructive, with connotations of dangerous female sexuality.

We could interpret this as two sides of the same argument: namely, that both the mother's and wet nurse's breast milk in Hepp's novel become corrupted by being turned from an original, or natural, purpose, the same purpose that sanctifies Marianne's milk in *Fécondité*. Catherine Toubin-Malinas has argued that, in *Fécondité*, Zola "raises human sexuality to the level of a magical rite, exorcising both the fear of the womb which becomes the creator of worlds, and also the terror of the female sex, which becomes the tabernacle of the religion of fecundity" (1986, 44).[93]

While Zola may have found a way to neutralize male fears of female sexuality through the sanctity of maternal breast-feeding, I would argue that Hepp's representation of mother's milk reflects unmitigated terror at the spectacle of both the selfish aristocratic mother and the evil lower-class wet nurse. Despite their endless rhetoric on the virtues of maternal breast-feeding, Hepp and many other authors of his time seem to find the representation of the act of breast-feeding both revolting and weirdly alluring. Without the framework of dutiful motherhood, the lactating breast becomes a symbol of uncontrollable female sexuality, as seen in the sexualization of the wet nurse in nineteenth- and even twentieth-century texts. A 1980 French manual on the history and practice of breast-feeding posited that "the relationship created by breast-feeding constitutes a type of possible jouissance that might risk escaping from both symbolization and social power" (Herbinet, 1980, 279).[94] Existing outside the boundaries of male control, breast milk becomes menacing in its irrepressible nature. Katrina Perry pointed out in a 2001 article on breast milk in *Fécondité* that "The omnipotent 'fleuve de lait' (river of milk) successfully transforms feminine sexuality into maternal servitude, but the image in its very abundance, and in its fluid nature, recalls unrepressed femininity" (2001, 98). A similarly uncontainable current of breast milk flows even more strongly through Hepp's text, creating a subtext of illicit maternal desire that defies the narrator's attempts to suppress it. Like Geneviève's milk, female sexuality explodes in the face of the reader, leaving behind a dangerous, yet oddly enticing, odor of sexual vice that subverts the author's ostensible moralistic message and likely ensured the novel's success.

Chapter 4

Breast-Feeding, Literature, and Politics in the Third Republic

Marilyn Yalom claimed that, during the Enlightenment, "modern Western democracies invented the politicized breast and have been cutting their teeth on it ever since" (1997, 105). As we saw in Chapter 1, breast-feeding became a political act during the French Revolution, as virtuous women were exhorted to lactate for the good of the Republic. During and after the birth of the Third Republic, in the last decades of the nineteenth century, politicians, writers, and moralists echoed those exhortations, reclaiming imagery of the breast-feeding mother as a symbol of Republican virtues. The late nineteenth century saw a resurgence in representations of nursing mothers, both positive and negative. Doctors of the Third Republic engaged in fiery debates about the social and medical consequences of the wet-nursing industry, publishing treatises on the mortality rates of infants sent out to the wet nurse as well as those of the wet nurses' own infants, to support legislation regulating the industry. Despite the massive propaganda efforts of the medical establishment, as well as technological and scientific advances such as pasteurization and the manufacture of safer and cheaper baby bottles, however, mercenary wet-nursing remained the norm among the upper and middle classes in Paris and other cities in France until after the Great War ended in 1918.[1]

The figure of the wet nurse appeared in stories and novels by Maupassant, Daudet, and others during this time, typically serving as morality tales that warned of the dire consequences of mercenary nursing. In his 1891 novel, *Another Woman's Milk*, Alexandre Hepp attempted to use the persuasive power of fiction to convince parents of the dangers inherent in hiring a wet nurse. His novel was touted by critics, journalists, and doctors of the time as an important warning that mothers should heed for the good of the nation, as was the more widely known Zola novel, *Fécondité*, published eight years later.

The propagandistic pro-natalist function of Zola's novel becomes apparent in the context of a France decimated by war and by a steadily decreasing birth rate. At such a time, the exhortation of women to fulfill their patriotic duty to procreate, reminiscent of the Revolutionary and Napoleonic periods, once again appeared in fiction and rhetoric. In this chapter, I will examine the relationship between the construction of the Third Republic and the rebirth of breast-feeding imagery in French literature, medicine, and politics, from the 1870s to the turn of the century.

The Public Outcry on the Fate of Wet Nurses' Infants

As the high mortality rate among infants sent out to country wet nurses became more widely known during the nineteenth century, the trend of hiring live-in wet nurses spread gradually from the wealthy classes to all levels of the bourgeoisie. More and more medical authorities began to recommend live-in wet nurses, citing lower mortality rates as well as various medical reasons why some wealthy women could not breast-feed. Even for doctors who opposed the wet-nursing industry, this seemed to be an acceptable compromise to safeguard the lives of wealthy urban babies, since it allowed for greater control of the wet nurse's diet and behavior (Fay-Sallois, 1980, 140; see also Millet-Robinet and Allix, 1897, 148).

Most moralists, politicians, and doctors prior to 1865 focused their efforts on reducing the mortality rate of infants whose mothers hired wet nurses, including indigent mothers who were forced to send their children out to nurse in order to earn a living. They paid little attention to the plight of the wet nurses' own children. Then, in 1865, the Academy of Medicine received a treatise called *On the Wet-Nursing Industry and Infant Mortality* by Dr. Charles Monot, mayor of a small town in the Morvan (Rollet, 1990). Doctor Monot wrote that two-thirds of the women who gave birth in his district between 1858 and 1864 departed for Paris as soon as they could walk, typically leaving their infants in the care of relatives who had no milk to feed them. According to Monot, for the wet nurses' newborns, "the mother's departure for Paris is often the death warrant for the child" (1867, 33).[2] Monot gathered data on the number of wet nurses' children who had died between 1858 and 1864 in the ten villages that made up his district. During those seven years, he counted 449 children who died after their mothers went to Paris to work as live-in wet nurses. Dr. Monot did not mince words in his assessment of the situation: "These are 449 victims of the wet-nursing industry, 449 premeditated infanticides […] 449 murders that are ignored and against which local authorities remain powerless" (47).[3] Monot's second book, in 1872, *On the Excessive Mortality of Children in Their First Year of Life, Its Causes and Means of Limiting It*, won a gold medal from the Academy of Medicine, and Monot was awarded the Legion of Honour for his work in 1884. Social historians Catherine Rollet and Fanny Fay-Sallois agree that Monot's effective use of statistics to highlight the high mortality rate among wet nurses' children, aided by increasing fears of depopulation, was instrumental in the passage of the Roussel Law in 1874, which mandated among other things that a wet nurse's child must be at least seven months old before the nurse could seek employment (Fay-Sallois, 1980, 117).

In the last few decades of the nineteenth century, a growing number of doctors, administrators, and moralists began advocating for the rights of children and the duty of the State to intervene with legal action whenever a child's welfare was endangered, regardless of socio-economic status. In 1869, Dr. Boudet gave an impassioned and influential speech to the Academy of Medicine on infant mortality in which he exclaimed: "The country is in danger!" (Rollet, 1990, 109).[4] A few years later, the well-respected *accoucheur* (obstetrician) Dr. Adolphe Pinard became known for the phrase, "The mother's milk belongs to the child," which he went so far as to have inscribed on the wall of the Maternity Hospital Baudelocque in Paris, where he practiced for more than twenty years (Cova, 1997, 43).[5] As an example of the growing movement legally to protect children's rights, social historian Catherine Rollet quotes Dr. Cambillard, who served as an inspector of *enfants assistés* (children receiving aid from the State) at the turn of the century: "The child, a human being and a member of society, must be preserved in his physical and moral integrity and […] public institutions have the right and the obligation to intervene in order to ensure his protection" (2001, 222).[6] The question remained, however: how could the government encourage, or perhaps obligate, mothers to breast-feed for the good of their children as well as the nation?

The passage of the Roussel Law in 1874 marked the first comprehensive attempt since the Revolutionary period to introduce the infant's legal right to its mother's milk into legislation. The law provided protection for children under two years of age who lived apart from their parents and were cared for by a third party, "for a salary." While the law still did not address the refusal of wealthy women to breast-feed their own children, article 8 specifically required women wishing to hire themselves out as wet nurses to prove that their own infant was at least seven months old, or, if not, that the infant was "nursed by a wet nurse who had no other nursling" (Pinard, 1908, 12).[7] Since these women could not afford to hire a wet nurse themselves, the law in effect required them to breast-feed their own infant for its first seven months of life.

However, according to medical authorities such as Dr. Pinard and Dr. Léon Petit, despite the efforts of legislators, this portion of the Roussel Law remained for the most part unenforced. Wet nurses all over France continued to make false statements regarding their newborns, and governmental supervision was spotty. Dr. Petit claimed that proper enforcement of article 8 would eventually lead to the death of the wet-nursing industry in France. In a speech based on his 1895 medical thesis entitled *The Child's Right to His Mother*, Petit said:

> Women who do not want to breast-feed will be forced to do so the day when the Roussel Law is no longer violated with impunity, as it is today. When wet nurses are no longer permitted to take jobs until after their own infants are at least seven months old, the bureaus will no longer be crowded; and the mercenary wet nurse, this immoral being who most often kills her own baby by depriving it of her milk in order to sell it, will disappear. I hope that, with all our efforts, mothers will understand their duty, and that the sacred rights of the child will finally be respected. (Leroy-Allais, 1900, 34–35)[8]

Rollet lists no fewer than thirty-three government directives (or *circulaires*), issued from 1874 to 1894, regarding various details of the application of the Roussel Law (1990, 135). The final *circulaire*, "The strict application of article 8," dated October 27, 1894, was initiated by Dr. Pinard and Henri Monod, director of Public Assistance. It stated, unambiguously, "that a woman's milk belongs not to her, but to her child; that she does not have the right to sell it as she pleases, and that if she can be allowed to give it to another's child, it is only when it can be legitimately presumed that her milk is no longer indispensable to the life and health of her own child (Pinard, 1908, 13).[9] Despite this insistence on mother's milk as the rightful legal property of the infant, Dr. Pinard confirmed in 1908 that article 8 continued to be largely ignored:

> And this fact proves yet again that, if it is good to change, to modify laws, it is especially indispensable to change, to modify customs. This law is not enforced, because the poor little abandoned children cannot complain, they cannot form a union, they must be content with uttering a few plaintive moans ... before they die. (Pinard, 1908, 13)[10]

In 1899, the enlightened Dr. Boutan in Zola's novel *Fécondité* outlines very clearly a program of political and social reform and support that sounds very much like Jacobus's "failed Enlightenment project of the French Revolution" a hundred years later:

> What was needed was general measures, laws to save the nation: to aid and protect women from the first difficult days of pregnancy, to relieve them of hard labor, to make them sacred; then to help them give birth, later, in peace, in secret if they wish, without asking anything of them other than being mothers; then, to care for, support mothers and children during convalescence, then during the long months of breast-feeding, until the day when, the child having been born, the woman can once more be a strong and healthy wife. It was only a matter of taking a series of precautions, creating houses, pregnancy refuges, secret maternity homes, convalescence clinics, not to mention protective laws or breast-feeding subsidies. There is only one way to combat the problem of the horrific waste of births, death snatching away so many newborns: prevention. (Zola, n.d., 385)[11]

The doctor takes Rousseau's remedy of women nursing their own children and applies practical measures to make this possible even in situations of extreme poverty. However, it would take another few decades for France to create wide-ranging social programs to protect and support pregnant and nursing women.

The failure of the Roussel Law to mitigate the suffering of nurslings is apparent in *Fécondité*. The protagonist, Matthieu, is appalled by the description of wet-nursing conditions in a village near Paris offered by Victoire, a young domestic servant. Victoire tells him of the horrific conditions in which nurslings are raised by their nurses, ranging from benign neglect to murder with intent, but then assures him that, before the Roussel Law, conditions were even worse, with the *meneuses* taking full advantage of the lack of supervision:

> I've heard my father tell about when the *meneuses*, in his day, would each bring back four or five babies at a time. Little packages that they wrapped up and carried under their arms. In train stations, they would line them up on the benches in the waiting room; one day, a *meneuse* from Rougemont left one behind, and there was a big to-do, because someone found the baby and it had died. And you should have seen, on the trains, what a pile of poor little creatures, wailing with hunger. [...] Often, some of them died, and they would take the little corpse off at the next station and bury it in the closest cemetery. You can imagine what state they arrived in, the ones who didn't die on the way. Where I'm from, we take much better care of the pigs, for we would surely never make them travel like that. My father said that it would draw tears from a stone... But now, there's more monitoring, the *meneuses* can only take one baby at a time. (Zola, n.d., 359)[12]

However, Victoire tells Matthieu that there are still all sorts of ways for the *meneuses* to cheat, bringing two nurslings each and asking other women on the train to carry more babies for them. She also claims that since the entire village profits from the wet-nursing industry, from the nurses themselves all the way to the mayor and the public health inspectors, the entire village turns a blind eye as the nurses and *meneuses* find ways to flout the Roussel law.

Catherine Toubin-Malinas has pointed out that Zola's portrayal of the wet-nursing industry absorbing entire villages, such as the fictional Rougemont in the novel, was based on extensive research of actual conditions of the period as well as the prevailing attitudes of French society toward the needless deaths of so many infants:

> From this contemporary documentation, followed by Zola with great care for accuracy and without the slightest exaggeration, it seems obvious that this deliberate massacre upset no one. Neither

the bourgeois ladies who doubled their own children's chances of death by entrusting them to live-in wet nurses, nor the nurses who knew that they had at least a 50/50 chance of never seeing their own children again, nor the peasant women who stuffed children with soup in grimy bottles and bowls, nor the *meneuses*, nor the midwives who knew perfectly well the fate that awaited the babies left in all the Rougemonts scattered across France. (Toubin-Malinas, 1986, 198)[13]

The role of Zola's novel as vehicle for social and political change could not be clearer. Twenty-five years after the passing of the Roussel Law, Zola depicts the wet-nursing industry in the same terms we see in the treatises leading up to 1874, as a clear and present danger to both women and children that puts at risk the very survival of France.

In light of the failure of the law to force underprivileged mothers to breast-feed their own children or to protect the nurslings sent to wet nurses, what more could be done to legislate lactation? Rachel Fuchs quoted a suggestion by an inspector of Public Assistance in 1891: "military service for all able-bodied men was compulsory. Therefore, maternal nursing should be obligatory for all robust and healthy mothers. This would be a way for her to give her blood to the nation" (1992, 169). Not surprisingly, no legislative action resulted from this suggestion. The Academy of Medicine continued its efforts to promote maternal breast-feeding into the twentieth century, as shown by a statement issued by that body in 1904: "Every mother has the duty to breast-feed her child. The child has a right to his mother's milk" (Pinard, 1908, 14).[14] In the same year, a new law for the protection of children reinstated the *secours d'allaitement* of a century earlier to enable poor mothers to stay home and nurse their children (Fuchs, 1992, 150). However, like the first such law issued by the Convention in 1793, this measure applied only to mothers seeking public assistance, not to all mothers equally.

In 1909, Dr. Sicard de Plauzoles published *Motherhood and the National Defense against Depopulation*, in which he made a strong argument for legally forcing women to breast-feed. Plauzoles based his argument on Article IV of the Declaration of the Rights of Man: "Liberty consists of being able to do anything that does not harm others: thus the exercise of each man's natural rights has as its limits those which ensure that the other members of society enjoy those same rights" (*Assemblée nationale*,

2021).[15] Plauzoles draws this conclusion: "it is evident that the mother in depriving the infant of her milk commits an act which harms him. She therefore does not have the right to commit it" (Sicard de Plauzoles, 1909, 265; quoted in Fuchs, 1992, 76). Again, however, no real legislative action resulted from this argument. In short, the various efforts to legislate lactation from the Revolution onward proved to be largely ineffectual.

In a series of *tableaux* called *Living Paris*, published in 1889, Ali Coffignon wrote: "It is the business of the State to protect nurslings and to preserve children, but the law and the administration can do nothing about maternal breast-feeding" (1889, 94).[16] This conclusion is supported by legal scholar Martine Herzog-Evans in *Breast-Feeding and the Law*, published in 2007:

> If the right to breast-feed could be the object of legislative protection without harm, the right to be breast-fed most certainly could not, since it would necessarily mean forcing mothers to breast-feed. Such a rule would constitute in any case an attack on individual liberties and on superior norms, and particularly on articles 16 of the Civil Code regarding the right to the respect of corporeal integrity. (Herzog-Evans, 2007, 18)[17]

Despite numerous recommendations by the World Health Organization and other international authorities on the health benefits of breast-feeding, recommendations that, as Herzog-Evans points out, have only a "power to incite," the breast-feeding rate in twenty-first-century France remains one of the lowest in Western Europe (2007, 13).

If successive governments have failed to ensure the right of an infant to its mother's milk, what other methods might be available to "resuscitate maternal integrity," as *La Fronde* put it in 1899? For the answer to this centuries-old question, we may turn to Émile Zola, whose 1896 article on depopulation in *Le Figaro* offered the solution of entrusting this effort "to moralists, writers and poets"[18] (2002–9, vol. 17, p. 432). In an article on Zola's reproductive politics, Andrew Counter has suggested that Zola's intention in conceiving the novel *Fécondité* was in fact to influence French morals by using the power of literature for the good of the nation. Counter quotes Zola's assertion that "everything would change, if one persuaded our pretty young ladies that nothing is as beautiful [...] as a large family" (2014, 197).[19] In Counter's view, Zola diverged here from previous generations of intellectuals who viewed literature as separate from politics, aesthetics existing for its own sake rather than for political purpose. By claiming that writers could change the world through the act of writing, Counter argues, Zola "does not mean to suggest that literature is more important than politics, but rather that literature *is* politics" (198). Certainly the late nineteenth-century popularity of the *roman à thèse*, a didactic type of novel that expounds upon a thesis, seemed to unite literature and politics, as Counter points out.

While Dr. Monot struggled to attract attention to the plight of wet nurses' infants, a poem by François Coppée, published in 1872, illustrated the negative effects on both the wet nurse's charge as well as her own child. Coppée's collection, *The Humble Ones*, was lauded by critics including Jules Lemaître (a good friend of Coppée) as a triumph of realism, a portrait of modern life in all its sordid details. Although Aimée Boutin has noted Coppée's "appeal to bourgeois sentimentalism," which was mocked by the young poets of the symbolist movement, Coppée remained one of the most popular and widely read authors of his time (2015, 108). His poetry and theatrical works as well as his social connections within the Parnasse movement and beyond earned him the rank of *Chevalier* of the Legion of Honour in 1876 and a place in the French Academy in 1884 (Francis, 1908, 671).

In *The Humble Ones*, Coppée included a poem called "The Wet Nurse," which tells the tragic story of a young woman from the country whose drunken and greedy husband forces her to leave for Paris and work as a wet nurse, despite her pleas to remain with their infant son.

> Horrible thought! To save their home,
> The cow, the chest, the mother had
> To leave her village, her modest house,
> Her son, his eyes still closed to the light,
> Who whimpered in the cradle, innocent babe!
> She had to sell her milk, alas! Dearer than her blood,
> And, humiliated by this servile act,
> In pain, she had to set out for the city. (Coppée, 1872, 6)[20]

Despite her conscientious efforts to fulfill her task in the city, the child in her charge weakens and dies. Her sadness is tempered with joy at the prospect of a reunion with her son, whom her husband has told her is thriving at home.

> The wet nurse wanted to go right home
> To the son whom she could feed today,
> To the country child, who was in good health. [...]
> Her long suffering is finally at an end.
> She will see her son! Finally! Oh Deliverance! (Coppée,
> 1872, 13–14)[21]

She bursts into her family's home, only to find her husband passed out drunk in a quiet house. Frantic, she begins searching everywhere for her child:

> And, in the shadows, among the old junk,
> Dirty, broken, covered in spiderwebs,
> Horrible object in the indignant mother's eyes
> That was thrown in this corner without remorse,
> The humble willow cradle of the little dead child.
> She fell down. The sacrifice was complete. (Coppée, 1872,
> 15)[22]

The woman goes mad with grief, and the poem ends with this heart-rending image:

> Ever since, you can see, in a Caen asylum,
> Staring at you with dry and burning eyes,
> A woman still young with hair gone white
> Who touches her own pallid breast
> And rocks an empty cradle with her foot. (Coppée, 1872,
> 16)[23]

Despite the poem's tragic tone and unfortunate ending, and unlike Hepp and Zola about twenty years later, Coppée does not indicate any authorial intent as to the moral of the story. Its place at the head of a collection of poems dealing with the everyday lives of ordinary people seems to frame it as just one of a series of unhappy tales taken from the author's observations of the suffering of the disadvantaged classes. In an 1889 retrospective of Coppée's life and work, critic Adolphe Lescure calls the wet nurse a "heroine and martyr to mercenary wet-nursing" but adds that "there is no bias; it is the subject that made it so" (1889, 159). I found no evidence that Coppée had any interest in the Society for the Protection of Children or that he knew Dr. Monot, although their acquaintance is likely given that they were inducted into the

Legion of Honour one year apart. The lack of authorial judgement and the sentimental appeal of Coppée's portrayal of the wet nurse as both innocent and unfortunate, along with the impact of poetic strategies such as rhyming "sacrifice" and "hospice" or "souffrance" and "délivrance," make this portrayal of the sacrifice of a wet nurse's child especially powerful. In sharp contrast to Hepp's and Zola's later representations of the wet nurse as an evil and soulless being whose motivation is purely selfish, Coppée's wet nurse is a victim of circumstance whose poverty and subjugation by a drunken husband force her to sell her milk for survival. Despite the redeemable nature of the wet nurse, however, the end result is the deaths of both her own child and the child she was hired to nurse. Even this sympathetic representation of a live-in wet nurse becomes an illustration of the dangers of the wet-nursing industry – for the wealthy Parisians as well as for the poor nurse and her family.

In *Another's Milk*, examined in detail in Chapter 3, the main character, Marianne, is an amoral, sexually promiscuous peasant woman and an unwed mother who goes to Paris to seek her fortune by selling her milk. Her abuse of the young boy in her charge leads to his complete moral destruction and serves as a clear warning to parents of the dangers of entrusting their children to a live-in wet nurse, no matter how closely supervised she may be. Marianne's own child plays only a minor role in the novel; when she leaves for Paris, her father sees her off, holding her infant son and a dirty baby bottle. Miraculously, despite his mother's complete lack of interest in him or his welfare, the child survives until five years later, when a messenger from the village arrives to tell Marianne that her son has died. The messenger is puzzled by her reaction:

> And nothing altered Marianne's features; she did not even seem surprised and the man who had brought her the news was left speechless. Really, her little baby had just been killed in a few days by the croup? Her little one! What little one? It was five years now since Marianne had come to the Baron's house, and never had she felt homesick, never had she felt a need to see or ask about her child; no, his life did not interest her at all; no, he did not exist for her, the child from back there! [...] Her child, the child back in the village? The one next to whom she would have been condemned to lead a miserable and unhappy life? Ah! He was forgotten, disowned, that child! (Hepp, 1891, 174)[24]

To the messenger's astonishment, Marianne refuses to return to the village with him to bury her son; the most she will agree to do is to give him money for the funeral. In this case, then, the death of the nurse's child serves as just one more indication of her immorality, one more justification for the reader to despise her. Hepp's novel shares with *Fécondité* the stated purpose of warning parents against the evils of wet nurses; while Hepp avoids the pitfalls of didactic propaganda a bit more successfully than Zola, the goal is essentially the same.

The most well-known of the late nineteenth-century literary portrayals of the dangers of wet-nursing is of course Émile Zola's 1899 novel *Fécondité*. The medical authority in the novel, Dr. Boutan, seems to echo the warnings of Dr. Monot, written thirty years earlier: "as for the live-in wet nurse, that's a shameful transaction, an incalculable source of harm, often even a double crime, the accepted double sacrifice of the mother's child and the wet nurse's child" (Zola, n.d., 387).[25] Through the eyes of the protagonist, Matthieu, we witness the doctor's examination of Marie Lebleu, a potential wet nurse holding her baby. "It was a boy, three months at the most, with a solid and strong look about him. For an instant, he raised his head to ask her: 'Is that baby yours, at least?' 'Oh! Sir! ... Where do you think I got him from?' 'Well, child, you could've borrowed one'" (399).[26]

Once the doctor approves of Marie, the intermediary (or *meneuse*), La Couteau, arranges to come to pick up Marie's baby to take him back to her village. Watching this, Matthieu predicts the child's death:

> Then, a shiver seized him when the *meneuse* turned to the beautiful, well-behaved infant that she was going to take off the nurse's hands. And he saw her again with the five others, at the Saint-Lazare station, disappearing, each taking with them a newborn, like harbingers of massacre and mourning. The roundup was starting again [...] with the threat this time of a double murder, as the doctor said, two infants in danger of dying, the mother's and the wet nurse's. (Zola, n.d., 402)[27]

Later, we hear La Couteau gossiping with another woman about the news that Marie's child has died. La Couteau's response both illustrates and condemns the casual attitude toward the fate of these children: "Such a beautiful baby! It's a wind that blows, what do you want. And besides, wet nurse's child, child of sacrifice (*enfant de nourrice, enfant de sacrifice*)" (423).[28] We learn that not only has Marie's own child died, but the wealthy Parisian child in her charge is failing as well. Matthieu's reaction to this double tragedy leaves little room for ambiguity:

> The sudden memory came back to him of his conversation with Boutan [...] the crime committed by both mothers, each risking her child's death, the lazy mother who was buying another's milk, the venal mother who was selling hers. He had a cold feeling inside ... And what would be the fate, what wind would blow for a society so badly formed and corrupt, sacrificing one or the other, or maybe both? Both people and things filled him with gloom and disgusted him. (Zola, n.d., 440–41)[29]

Matthieu brings the issue back to the corruption of late nineteenth-century society, which has strayed from traditional family values due to sloth and avarice. Zola's novel openly advocates for the elimination of the wet-nursing industry and the propagation of maternal breast-feeding; the plight of the nurses' children is only one part of the evidence toward that goal.

Author Léon Bloy in 1899 was reading Zola's *Fécondité* in installments in the newspaper, which he described as stories "that are exclusively about wet nurses who kill" (1899, 516).[30] Sick and tired of reading these depressing tales, Bloy lamented: "Oh François Coppée! [...] You know what a *mother* is! You know what the homeland means [...] and you know especially what it means to *write*!" (516–17).[31] While Bloy's epithet for Zola ("the Idiot," or "le Crétin") seems a bit extreme, it is widely agreed that *Fécondité* is far from his finest literary achievement. Frederick Hemmings, in his 1953 book on Zola, wrote: "Judged purely as a work of art, *Fécondité* is an excellent example of the aberrations into which 'committed literature' is apt to tempt the unwary" (1953, 280). In his 1973 book on *Fécondité*, David Baguley stated that the novel exists primarily as propaganda against the wet-nursing industry, and the plot and characters remain secondary considerations (1973, 181).

Jacques Noiray pointed out that in Zola's later works, including the *Evangels* (to which *Fécondité* belongs), "the characters are merely the incarnation of an idea" (1993, 151–52).[32] We know that the author's intent as he wrote *Fécondité* was to promote what he saw as the essential values of family, work, and redemption that would reconstruct the French nation and ensure its survival. Furthermore, Zola believed that only literature had the power to change people's behavior. In his 1896 article on depopulation, in *Le Figaro*, Zola wrote: "And this is why, legislators seeming to me to be powerless, I would like this task to be entrusted to moralists, writers and poets" (2002–9, vol. 17, p. 432).[33] In 1899, in an interview for the feminist newspaper *La Fronde*, Zola expressed his frustration with French women who seemed to ignore all the good advice of doctors and moralists: "their calculations are wrong, for breast-feeding tires the mother but does not harm her; on the contrary, it is useful to the entire race" (Lefébure, 1899, 1).[34]

In *The Shadow of the Second Mother: Nurses and Nannies in Theories of Infant Development*, Prophecy Coles points out that the figure of the wet nurse is often neglected in our literary and social history. Coles writes: "Whichever way we look at the wet nurse she inhabits an ambiguous place in the hearts of those she has fed and in the minds of those who have employed her" (2015, 37). This psychological ambiguity may explain the relatively few representations of the wet nurse's loss of her child, since most producers of literary works in nineteenth-century France were upper- and middle-class men whose own survival may well have depended on the willingness of a lower-class wet nurse to sell the milk intended for her own child. While Hepp's and Zola's literary wet nurses seem to be one-dimensional symbols of corruption, Coppée presents a much more nuanced image of a virtuous wet nurse oppressed by fate. All of the nurses' children, however, are doomed.

The Personal is Political: Marianne's Breasts and the Third Republic

As we have seen, Mary Jacobus has shown that the iconography of the Republic that replaced the symbols of the *ancien régime* in the French imaginary consisted primarily of a bare-breasted (often breast-feeding) female figure who became an allegory for Liberty and eventually for the French nation (1995, 222).[35] In this section, we will see how this allegorical female figure that came to be known as Marianne took on the role of symbolizing the values of the new French republic and its promise to feed and nurture all citizens of France. We will then examine the role of Marianne as political symbol during the Third Republic, particularly in the final decade of the nineteenth century.

Perhaps the most well-known representation of the female embodiment of the ideals of the French Revolution today is Eugène

Delacroix's 1830 painting, *Liberty Leading the People*, which, contrary to popular belief, represents the July revolution of 1830 against the restored Bourbon monarchy rather than the revolution of 1789 (Yalom, 1997, 122). The bare-breasted allegory of the Republic or of Liberty depicted in numerous paintings, statues, engravings, and public displays both during and after the Revolutionary period came to symbolize the struggling ideals of the Revolution: liberty, equality, and fraternity, particularly as those ideals came under attack from the various undemocratic regimes throughout the nineteenth century.

While the female allegory embodying the French nation experienced a rebirth with each successive iteration of the French republic, it did not bring with it a more enlightened view of women's participation in the public sphere. In Jacobus's analysis of the Revolutionary period's representation of "the State as Mother Republic," she underlines the contradictions between men's strategic use of the allegorical figure of bare-breasted Liberty wearing the Phrygian or liberty cap and the possibility of real, cap-clad Frenchwomen participating in political life. The latter created much anxiety among Revolutionary leaders, including Chaumette, president of the Paris Commune in 1793, who responded to a delegation of such women as follows: "It is horrible, it is contrary to all the laws of nature for a woman to want to make herself a man. [...] Is it to men that Nature confided domestic cares? Has she given us breasts to breast-feed our children?" (1995, 218–19). Jacobus diagnoses this as fear of "the unmanning of Revolutionary men" by women who refused to remain in the private sphere and nurse their children, as was their prescribed duty (219).

Jacobus also sees in the image of the bountiful, breast-feeding figure of the French nation that dominated Revolutionary iconography, "the great, failed Enlightenment project of the French Revolution, the proposed abolition of the poor altogether by way of a system of legislated poor relief, which would have done away with the *enfant trouvé* and the wet nurse alike" (222). This project of feeding the hungry and eliminating both poverty and the child neglect resulting from it was reflected in the various attempts to legislate breast-feeding from the last decade of the eighteenth century to the early twentieth century.

This ideal of State assistance to the poor, particularly to poor mothers and infants, seemed to experience a resurgence with each reiteration of the French Republic. On the eve of the 1848 revolution that would bring down Louis-Philippe's government and result in the establishment of the Second Republic, historian Jules Michelet published *The People* (*Le Peuple*), a lyrical account of the tensions and challenges facing the average French citizen in the 1840s. In his words on the importance of the motherland (*la matrie*), embodied by the Republic, we hear the echo of this Revolutionary vision:

> If your mother cannot feed you, if your father mistreats you, if you are naked, if you are hungry, come, my son, the doors are wide open, and France is on the threshold to embrace and welcome you. This great mother will never be ashamed to care for you as a wet nurse would, she will prepare a soldier's soup for you with her own heroic hands, and if she had nothing else in which to wrap your little limbs numbed with cold, she would just as soon tear off a piece of her flag. (Michelet, 1877, 302–3)[36]

Not only does the Republic provide nourishment and care for all citizens of France: for Michelet, she also represents the source of life itself. Michelet compares the Republic–mother to God the Father of all humanity, source of all life, with a paraphrase of Acts 17:28: "In eâ movemur et sumus," or, "In this we move and have our being" (1877, 258 n, 1).[37]

Following the 1848 revolution, the new government held a contest to create a visual representation of the "face of the Republic" (Agulhon and Bonté, 1992, 28). Honoré Daumier, known primarily as a caricaturist for the satirical newspaper *Le Charivari*, submitted a painted sketch of a large, severe-looking, bare-breasted woman wearing a Phrygian cap and nursing two young boys. His image of the Republic appears to be an illustration of Michelet's passionate description in *The People* of "a powerful nurse who breast-feeds us by the millions" (1877, 258 n. 1).[38] Although Michelet and Daumier did not meet until 1852 (Escholier, 1965, 85), Daumier could very well have read Michelet's book, which sold a thousand copies in Paris on the first day of its publication in 1846 (Michelet, 1973, n.p.). The sketch was placed eleventh in the contest and Daumier was invited to submit a more polished, full-sized version, which he never did (Poirrier, 2021, unpag.). A contemporary critic called Daumier's Republic "fertile, serene and glorious," and the boy reading at her feet was also much admired.[39] Here was the promise of the original republic as established during the Revolutionary period, of a nation dedicated to feeding, caring for, and educating all its (male) citizens without exception. Despite the unfinished state of the painting, Daumier's image continues to capture the imagination of both art historians and the French public and remains an important part of the visual vocabulary of French Republican nationalism today; the painting itself hangs in the Musée d'Orsay in Paris, whereas the painting by Jean Lyon Gérôme that won the contest, of a cold and static, fully clothed woman, lies forgotten in the storage rooms of the Petit Palais (Escholier, 1965, 167). Although today we refer to Daumier's strong female figure as Marianne, the allegory of the republic did not acquire that name until a few years later, around 1850, when Marianne became an underground symbol of left-wing resistance to the conservative government of President Louis-Napoleon prior to his coup d'état (Agulhon and Bonté, 1992, 34–35).

In his book on the collective psychology of France as seen in the figure of Marianne, physician Paul Trouillas described the lasting appeal of the unfinished Daumier painting as stemming from its illustration of the Republic's embodiment of social and economic equality:

> [A] Marianne-Mother opens her powerful and generous bosom to children who take nourishment there. The symmetry in this magnificent work introduces the idea of Equality naturally. It is possible, but not certain, that the two "children of the Republic" evoke the principle of social classes. In any case, the idea of generosity and of economic equity that we had suggested are illustrated perfectly here. The breast is the power to give a shared social and political benefit. (Trouillas, 1988, 251)[40]

The breast of the Republic symbolizes the government's role of caring for its citizens, much in the same way it did during the Revolutionary period.

Having gone underground during the Second Empire, along with the Republican movement, Marianne became a centerpiece of the French public imagination again in 1870, with the declaration of the Third Republic. In 1889, for the hundredth anniversary of the French Revolution, hundreds of statues of Marianne as the embodiment of the Republic were erected all over France, including the one by Jules Dalou still standing in the *place de la Nation* in Paris. Most included the now-familiar symbols of the bared breast and the Phrygian cap, in addition to other symbols borrowed from antiquity and Masonic tradition, such as the scales of justice (Agulhon and Bonté, 1992, 62).

At the same historical moment, with the end of the Franco-Prussian war and its perceived decimation of France's population as described by the relatively new field of demographic statistics, many public authorities and intellectuals in France felt there was a dire need to produce more and better citizens to repopulate the nation. These fears only increased as the century progressed, with numerous calls from doctors, moralists, and government officials for French women to have more children. As we have seen, Jacques Bertillon, both a trained doctor and a statistician, founded the National Alliance for the Increase of the French Population in 1896, the same year that Zola wrote an article entitled "La Dépopulation" for *Le Figaro* (Bertillon, 1897). Much of this rhetoric was aimed at the responsibility of mothers to forego the wet nurse and breast-feed their own children, for the good of the Republic.

Why was this responsibility perceived to rest almost entirely with women? The idea of women's duty to support the nation by making babies was far from new in the late nineteenth century, as explained in previous chapters. In her biography of pioneering midwife Madame du Coudray, who strove to combat infant mortality after a series of wars in the seventeenth century, historian Nina Rattner Gelbart wrote: "Women's bodies have as a result gradually come to be thought of as a kind of national property, somehow coming under the stewardship and use rights of the state, counted on to ensure the regular fecundity of society" (1998, 91). Rousseau's *Emile, or on Education* both reiterated this concept and extended it to the maternal breast, stating that if mothers would only nurse their own infants, "the State would be repopulated" (1964, 18). Throughout the nineteenth century, the various governments of France (from empires to monarchies to republics) all took the official position that French mothers should breast-feed their own infants, while also continuing to pass laws to regulate the existing wet-nursing industry. Most governmental attempts to encourage, or even to obligate, mothers to breast-feed their children went hand in hand with the concept of public assistance born during the Revolution.[41]

The Society of Maternal Charity, created as a private organization in 1784 and nationalized by Napoleon in 1811,[42] continued to receive regular government subsidies throughout the years of Restoration, the July monarchy, the Second Empire, and the early years of the Third Republic, thanks to a decree in October 1814 guaranteeing a subvention of 100,000 francs to maternal societies throughout France that remained in effect until its abrogation in 1882 (Adams, 2010, 175). However, such aid remained restricted to mothers who were considered morally deserving (in other words, married or widowed). More unusual were the few private charitable organizations that operated outside the bounds of Catholic and conventional morality. In 1876, feminist Marie Bécquet de Vienne founded the Society of Maternal Breast-Feeding for the purpose of providing financial support to indigent mothers, regardless of religion or marital status, to enable them to breast-feed their babies. Bécquet de Vienne proved to be a vocal and effective advocate for poor mothers and infants in the last decades of the century; as she wrote in the *Philanthropic Review* in 1897: "Assistance is the child's due. He has a right to entire, complete and permanent protection" (1897, 12).[43] Repeating the now-familiar Republican rhetoric of the good of the nation, she postulated the infant's right to its mother's milk in no uncertain terms: "It seems to me that breast-feeding one's children is for our country of the greatest interest and the first duty. It is not the draping in the flag that Michelet evokes that the child demands, it is his mother's milk to which he has a right" (561).[44] Interestingly, many late nineteenth-century French feminists strongly advocated maternal breast-feeding; an 1899 article in the feminist newspaper *La Fronde* called it a "maternal duty" as well as "a question that is vital to our nation" (Cova, 1997, 37).

From the 1860s on, government-subsidized aid largely concentrated on addressing the infant mortality rate by taking measures to increase the survival rate of young children. Accordingly, the General Administration of Public Assistance, founded under the Second Republic in 1849 and still in existence today, renamed its aid to parturient mothers, previously called the "assistance to prevent abandonment," the *secours d'allaitement*, or "breast-feeding assistance" (Fuchs, 1992, 141). A report of the General Council of the Department of the Seine in 1882 claimed that, thanks to the *secours d'allaitement*, mortality among infants nursed by their mothers was 19 percent lower than that of infants in general and that approximately 500 babies had been saved the previous year who might otherwise have died. The report recommends increased vigilance "to force mothers who accept this assistance to nurse their children themselves"[45] (*Conseil général du département de la Seine*, 1882, 625–26). As with all the previously mentioned legislative measures, however, this enforcement applied only to indigent mothers who accepted financial assistance from the State; it did not change anything for wealthy women or for women who sold their milk as a means of survival. Émile Zola believed that the only way to improve the situation of infants in France was to touch the hearts and minds of French parents through persuasive arguments presented in the guise of fiction. What interests us here is how two novels discussed in previous chapters, Zola's *Fécondité* and Hepp's *Another's Milk*, used the political representation of the Republic, Marianne, as a tool for instigating social and political change. This use of literature to effect social and political change can be seen in the portrayal of the plight of wet nurses' children in Hepp and Zola's turn-of-the-century novels.

Marianne in Zola's *Fécondité*: The Triumph of the Virtuous Motherland

Of the two novels mentioned, Zola's 1899 novel *Fécondité* is by far the best known and most often cited as an example of literary personification of the Republic. Numerous scholars have written of the Republican symbolism of the heroine's name. In his 1989 book on the history of Marianne as the allegory of the French Republic, historian Maurice Agulhon chose to mention only two literary representations. The first was *Marianne*, a one-act play by Alexandre Picot, produced at the Odéon Theater in Paris in September 1892, and long since forgotten, which ended with the patriotic cry of "Long live the Republic!" (Agulhon, 1989, 181). The second was Zola's *Fécondité*, whose heroine Marianne is described by Agulhon as a "goddess of a pantheistic religion of Nature and Life, very clearly opposed to the sterile religion of Catholicism" (183). In response to the possible objection that Zola named her Marianne by pure coincidence, Agulhon writes:

> One would have a hard time believing that Zola did not make a meaningful choice, since Marianne's husband, Matthew, has three brothers named Mark, Luke, and John (the four Evangelists) and that their last name is *Froment* (or "wheat," symbol of an agricultural fertility just as exulted throughout the novel as that of men). (Agulhon, 1989, 183)[46]

Carmen Mayer-Robin, in a 2000 article in *Excavatio*, made an exhaustive and persuasive case for Marianne's character as an embodiment of Republican virtues. After highlighting the role of Marianne in Zola's novel as giver of life and milk to the Froment family, and thereby to the French nation, she goes on to show that by the end of the novel Marianne seems to be transformed into a marble bust reminiscent of those found in every French town after the centenary of the Revolution:

> All white too, her face softened, lit by the last light of dawn under fine silk headbands, she was like one of those sacred marble statues whose features were worn down by time without destroying the tranquil splendor of life, a fertile Cybele, rediscovered in her firm plan, brought back to life in broad daylight. (Zola, n.d., 1006)[47]

As Mayer-Robin points out, Zola's Marianne represents the more conservative mid- to late-century version of the Republic, in which a less controversial crown or headband replaced the red Phrygian bonnet of the Revolution (2000, 74). Agulhon describes this stately and static figure, as seen on the official postage stamp of the Second Republic issued in 1849, as "crowned with an ear of wheat, which gave it the title, well known among philatelists still today, of 'Ceres-style' stamp, from the name of the Roman goddess of the harvest"[48] (1992, 32). An article in the art journal *L'Artiste*, of March 12, 1848, only weeks after the declaration of the Second Republic, stated that the Republic "shall not wear a red bonnet. She will not be an army cook, but a fertile mother, serene and glorious, who will have celebrations and smiles for her children" (Agulhon and Bonté, 1992, 32).[49]

This description in 1848 seems to be made for Zola's Marianne of 1899, who is most often portrayed at rest and smiling, either pregnant or nursing her latest baby. For instance, at the beginning of book two of the novel, we see the heavily pregnant Marianne through the eyes of her adoring husband as they both wake up one morning:

> In the patch of bright sunlight that covered the bed in a golden glow, she exuded good health, strength, and hope. Her thick dark hair had never flowed so powerfully down the nape of her neck; her wide eyes had never smiled with a more courageous joy. And, with her face of goodness and love, marked by such a solid and healthy propriety, she was fecundity itself, the good goddess with radiant skin, a perfect body, and a sovereign nobility.
>
> A sense of veneration came over him. He worshipped her, like a pious soul placed in the presence of his God, at the threshold of mystery. (Zola, n.d., 154)[50]

Here we see Marianne as the symbol of many things: fertility foremost, but also religious fervor and the importance of motherhood as a social force for change. Once she gives birth, her milk becomes synonymous with life itself, as seen in oft-repeated poetic tributes to "the flood of milk flowing through the world, the flood of eternal life for the eternal harvest of souls" (346).[51]

Katrina Perry has analyzed the lyrical nature of Zola's passages praising Marianne and fertility, which stand out because Zola was "not generally known for his attention to poetic details." Perry called Zola's lengthy descriptions of nature "oceanic," with long "rolling sentences" that crescendo and ebb to imitate the rhythms of nature (2001, 97). According to Mayer-Robin, as the novel progresses, the character Marianne is transformed from a real, flesh and blood mother nursing her many children into an abstract representation of the Republic that Matthieu, the protagonist, can "conjure [...] up in moments of moral difficulty" (2000, 74). Agulhon's history of Marianne as symbol of the French Republic confirms that she is often seen with one or both breasts bared, particularly after 1848, when more conservative "legalist" Republicans would "prefer an opulent bosom, more maternal, promising generosity and abundance" (Agulhon and Bonté, 1992, 39).[52]

Zola then projects this concept of the Republic as fertile mother onto the colonizing discourse of his day, as Marianne's offspring go forth to people the "new France" of the African colonies. Dominique, the prodigal grandson returning from Africa, recounts his family's conquest of their vast African acreage as a triumph of fertility, both of the land itself and of the French "race": "In the colonies, there is no more fertile race than the French race, which seems to have become sterile on its ancient ground. And we will multiply, and we will fill up the world" (Zola, n.d., 1027).[53] As Jacques Noiray wrote, "The reservoir of flowing milk takes with it in its irresistible expansion the multiplying brood of the Froment family as they go forth to conquer the world" (1993, 145).[54] In a 2006 article on the African chapters of *Fécondité*, Mayer-Robin noted that the same Zola who defends Dreyfus and glorifies Marianne as a symbol of republican progress also "concludes this novel, which promises the forward march of humanity, by excluding the African from the divinely dreamed up 'cité unique de paix, de verité et de justice' ['unique city of peace, truth, and justice']" (2006, 13). Like most men of his day, Zola saw no contradiction there; he wrote in the conclusion of the novel of the "docile Negroes," the "ferocious" natives motivated by religious fanaticism, and the "terrible problem of Islam" (n.d., 1025–26) facing the French colonists in Africa, before ending on a note of colonial optimism: "Beyond the seas, the milk had flowed, from the old land of France, to the immensities of virgin Africa, the young and massive France of tomorrow" (1038–39).[55]

For Mayer-Robin, Zola's novel lays out "a political economy, where the wealth and fecundity of liberated families spreads outward toward the entire nation and all of humanity" (2000, 76). At the center of this economy is Marianne, mother and source of all life, symbol of a Republic created in the image of Zola's utopian vision, a government that cares for all its citizens and exercises its benign authority just as the elderly Marianne Froment does at the end of the novel. This cult of Marianne replaces both government and religion in Zola's utopian future, with the goddess of fertility as deity and (white male) humanity worshipping at her feet. Zola uses the ideal of Marianne to represent, not the corrupt Third Republic of his day that had condoned the condemnation of Dreyfus, but the ideal Republic as it should be, liberated from the petty politics and partisanship of the late nineteenth century. In this way, the nursing breast becomes a symbol of the male author's utopian fantasy.

Marianne in Hepp's *Another's Milk*: The Corruption of the Republic

While Zola attempted to idealize the Republic in his depiction of Marianne, another author a few years earlier had used Marianne's symbolic significance to support his critique of the wet-nursing industry as well as of the republican government that allowed it to continue. In Chapter 3, we examined Alexandre Hepp's 1891 novel *Another's Milk* as an illustration of the fear of uncontrolled female sexuality. As an active journalist during the decades surrounding the hundredth anniversary of the Revolution, including a stint as editor-in-chief of the Republican-leaning newspaper *Le Voltaire*, Hepp would have been all too aware of the political resonance of the name Marianne. Much as caricaturists used Marianne as a tool to critique the government, Hepp's choice of the name Marianne for the corrupt and morally bankrupt wet nurse in *Another's Milk* could be interpreted as a political commentary on the state of the Third Republic.

In the first chapter of Hepp's novel, the pregnant Baroness Geneviève Davin describes the wet nurse at the center of this *roman à these* as a beautiful young woman with lovely white skin whose milk tastes appetizing and sweet (1891, 30). The reader learns that the wet nurse comes from a village called Sennelisse, two hours from Paris, and her name is Marianne Escarbier. Baron Michel Davin protests that wet nurses are forced into their line of work by weakness, misfortune or vice, all of which would have a negative effect on their beloved son (26). Geneviève counters that this particular wet nurse "looks innocent, placid, immaculate," despite her status as an unwed mother, and therefore that she must have gotten pregnant the first time she was with a man (29). Her unmarried status puts Marianne solidly outside the bounds of acceptable morality, reinforcing Michel's concerns about vice and weakness. Interestingly, although they are on opposite sides of the argument about employing wet nurses, both Michel and Geneviève use similar animalistic terms to describe them. Michel refers to wet nurses as "a herd," while Geneviève describes the doctor "milking" Marianne, saying that these women "are not of the same species as we are" (26; 30). To herself, Geneviève justifies her refusal to nurse their child by the example of her friends who all "possess" a ribbon-wearing wet nurse, because, after all, "we are mothers, not milk cows!" (16).

When we first meet Marianne in Chapter 2, she is tidying herself after having had sex with a young man from her village on the night before her departure for Paris. She has multiple sexual encounters that night, offering a blatant contrast with Geneviève's description of her as innocent and pure. In addition to her sexual promiscuity, Marianne speaks avidly of the money she will make as a wet nurse, revealing her greed as well as her lubricity. Her lack of interest in her own infant as she boards the coach for Paris completes the tableau; she holds him for a moment but refuses to give him her precious breast milk, which is worth so much money in Paris, offering him a dirty baby bottle instead (56–57).

Unlike some of the negative portrayals of wet nurses in French literature that we have examined previously, Marianne is not neglectful, ignorant, or intoxicated, at least at the outset. She is, on the contrary, extremely attentive to her duties and seems quite dedicated to the well-being of little Maurice Davin. As we have seen, Marianne's corruption of Maurice stems not from neglect, but from a combination of avarice and weakness, warped by her own situation as a young single woman deprived of any other sexual outlet. Marianne's cautionary tale begins with her lack of conventional morality and ends with her sexual initiation of her young charge, followed by her prostitution, drunkenness, and finally her death. Her faults stem not from individual malice, but rather from systemic problems with the wet-nursing industry, which places ignorant peasant women with no moral standards and no education in a position of power over an innocent upper-class child while encouraging their tendency toward avarice (with money and gifts) and vice (by denying them access to legitimate sexual partners). Given his subjection to such a system, young Maurice's moral destruction seems inevitable from the moment Michel cedes to his wife's insistence on hiring a wet nurse.

The moral of the story is unambiguous from the first page of the novel, with its dedication: "To the mother who breast-feeds, who does not want any intermediary between you and your son: this novel is your triumph, and I dedicate it to you." In the prologue, the author claims that the novel is based on a true story. He also states that he hopes mothers who read this book will think twice about hiring a mercenary wet nurse, because this sort of misfortune happens every day (i–ii). Here, too, the author insists on the universality of this type of abuse, hoping that his frank portrayal will prevent future crimes from occurring.

Much less clear is the author's reason for choosing the name Marianne for his depraved wet nurse. To better understand the possible explanations for this choice, it may be useful to examine Hepp's professional trajectory in the years prior to 1890. Described by some literary scholars as a naturalist disciple of Zola (Marchal, 1998, 468; Béthléem, 1928, 125), Hepp wrote *Another's Milk* at the height of his journalistic and literary career, after his arrival in Paris from his native Alsace a little more than a decade earlier. In an article for *Le Figaro* of July 10, 1888, Parisis (pseudonym of journalist Émile Blavet) describes Hepp's rise to fame as one of the most rapid he had ever seen (Blavet, 1888, n.p.). According to Parisis, Hepp began by publishing a modest article on François Coppée's *Madame de Maintenon* in the republican newspaper *Le Voltaire*, never imagining that he would soon take over from Zola as *Le Voltaire*'s theatre critic before becoming its editor in chief. In the meantime, he became known throughout Paris for his witty and scathing chronicles of everyday life in the capital, which he later published in several volumes. Parisis praises the "sparkling, picturesque style full of imagery" in Hepp's chronicles and then offers a sympathetic review of Hepp's novel *L'Epuisé* (*The Exhausted Man*), the story of a man who inherits syphilis from his father, first published in serial form in *Le Matin* until the editor suspended publication after the twelfth installment due to its offensive nature. Hepp refused to moderate the graphic content of his novel for the newspaper, stating that the novel "will appear just as I conceived it," a "sincere and chaste work" that contains "brutal truths" about its subject. This "profession of faith" earns the reviewer's praise for both the man and the author (Blavet, 1888, n.p.).

A tribute to Hepp in *Les Annales littéraires* following his death in 1924 referred to his invention of the genre of the chronicle: "brief notes inspired by the chance encounters of current events, brief pages where he described both big and small events of the day in the manner of an informed psychologist writing with amiable irony" ("Les Deuils, 1924). After Hepp left his full-time job with the *Voltaire*, he wrote for numerous other Parisian periodicals of the time, including the conservative monarchist newspaper *Le Gaulois*. In fact, two journalist colleagues (Aurélien Scholl and Henri Baüer) mocked Hepp in 1887 for having sold his soul by publishing articles in quick succession in both the republican-leaning *Le Voltaire* and the conservative, Catholic *Le Gaulois*, with the result that Hepp challenged them both to a duel. The matter was settled after they printed a retraction, but the incident raises questions about Hepp's political views in a period of turbulent political affiliations ("La Colère de M. Hepp," 1887, 2).

On May 10, 1890, in an interview for *Le Matin* about his latest novel, *Chaos*, Hepp told the reporter that he was already hard at work on his next novel, *Another's Milk*. He also revealed that he was preparing to send off the requisite five volumes for his candidacy for the Montyon Literary Prize, awarded by the French Academy to authors whose work proved useful to moral standards ("Prix Montyon," 2020). The interviewer compared Hepp's aspirations for the literary prize to Zola's candidacy to the French Academy that year, both of which were destined to fail, saying that these "audacious" new authors and "vigorous talents" hoped to "infuse new blood into this ancient body" (referring to the Academy) ("Chez Monsieur Hepp," 1890). A few years later, in 1898, Hepp would also be a founding member of the *Ligue de la Patrie* (League of the Fatherland), a conservative group led by writer and member of the French Academy Jules Lemaître, aimed at uniting the various factions in favor of prosecuting well-known Jewish army officer Alfred Dreyfus (known as the *anti-Dreyfusards*) (Conner, 2014, 160). The *Ligue de la Patrie Française* is considered a forerunner of present-day right-wing nationalism. Many Academicians supported its cause, such as François Coppée, Paul Bourget, and Jules Verne, as well as numerous well-known painters of the day including Degas and Renoir. A coalition of moderate and fervently anti-Semitic nationalists, the *Ligue* dissolved after just a few years (Conner, 2014, 160). Hepp's presence as one of its original founders could indicate a schism with Zola, who became famous for his January 1898 article defending Dreyfus in the newspaper *L'Aurore*, with the eye-catching headline "J'accuse!" (Zola, 1898, 1).

Based on Hepp's move from republican to more conservative, Catholic periodicals, and his adherence to the conservative nationalist *Ligue*, we can speculate that his use of the name Marianne in *Another's Milk* represents a political commentary on the weakness and vice of the Third Republic. Maurice Agulhon's analysis of the widespread use of Marianne to represent opposing political views in the press during this period seems pertinent here: "In the form of a feminine image, finally, Marianne, beautified and vilified depending on the opinion being defended, conveniently represents the government in political caricature, which was now flourishing freely" (1973, 18).[56] Reminiscent of caricatures of Marianne in the opposition press of the late nineteenth century, Hepp's Marianne, with her vices and inherent weaknesses, symbolizes the corruption and moral depravity of the French Republic. Once again, the lactating breast becomes a reflection of the political ideals of a male author and a tool to convince others of the evils of wet-nursing as well as of the decadence of the government then in power.

Conclusion

On February 15, 1901, Parisians flocked to the Théâtre Antoine to see the new play by Eugène Brieux, *Les Remplaçantes* (*The Surrogates*). Brieux's didactic plays had been a staple of the theater's naturalist repertoire since the early 1890s, and audiences seemed to respond well to his somewhat preachy style. In *Les Remplaçantes*, a village woman's family pressures her into leaving her husband and newborn child to go sell her milk in Paris. She finds employment with a wealthy Parisian family, who dote on her as she nurses their child. Then a telegram arrives bearing news that the nurse's own child has fallen ill. As her employers debate whether to tell her, a physician from the countryside, Dr. Richon, played to great acclaim by theater director André Antoine, pronounces a long tirade on the perils and consequences of the wet-nursing industry. The wet nurse learns the news, abandons her charge in Paris, and returns home, where she saves her husband from his profligate ways and nurses their child back to health (R.E.B., 1901, 465).

Critics panned the play as unoriginal, seemingly unfinished, and overly moralizing (see, for example, du Tillet, 1901, 250–52; Charpentier, 1908, 457–80). One critic called it a "play with a moral; it's mostly a moral, and it is regrettable that the play itself is neglected" (R.E.B., 1901, 465).[1] Nevertheless, *Les Remplaçantes* was a great success, with 116 performances in 1901 and reprises in the three following years as well, making it the longest-running of all his plays (Thomas, 1914, 71). Due in large part to the popularity of his work with the general public, Brieux was elected to the prestigious French Academy in 1909, an honor that Zola never achieved despite multiple attempts. Just as Zola hoped to change hearts and minds through the persuasive influence of literature, Brieux intended to use theatre as a way of educating the French public on serious issues of the day. As Brieux himself explained in a speech to the American Academy of Arts and Letters in 1914: "I wish through the theatre not only to make people think, to modify habits and facts, but still more to bring about laws which appear to me desirable" (v). Dr. Richon's monologue on wet-nursing in the play, which one critic called a "dramatic lecture" (Herold, 1908, 241), mentions the Roussel Law of 1870 and the need to better enforce it for the welfare of French children. Thirteen years later, Brieux claimed that *Les Remplaçantes* had improved and even saved lives with its anti-wet-nursing message (Thomas, 1914, v).

At least one contemporary critic noted in early 1901 the similarities between Brieux's play and Hepp's *Another's Milk* from a decade earlier (R.E.B., 1901, 465). A few months after the debut of *Les Remplaçantes*, Brieux completed another play called *Les Avariés* (*The Damaged Ones*) addressing the problem of syphilis, which the censors banned from the stage due to offensive content before it could open. Shortly thereafter, on November 5, 1901, Alexandre Hepp published an open letter to Brieux in *Le Figaro*, accusing the playwright of copying the substance of Hepp's novels of a decade earlier, *Le Lait d'une autre* and *L'Épuisé* (*The Worn Out Man*). Several other periodicals reproduced the letter, including *The Echo of Paris*, which published an interview with Hepp the following day on the outcome of the dispute under the provocative title, "The Hepp–Brieux Incident" (Hauser, 1901). In the interview, Hepp claimed that he was "the first man of letters to have written literary works about the dangers of wet nurses, about the danger of men injured by love." According to Hepp, Brieux took these two subjects that belonged to him and "popularized" them, and Hepp insisted that Brieux admit it (Hauser, 1901).[2] Fortunately, Brieux reviewed the evidence and publicly conceded that Hepp had treated these subjects first, resolving the conflict with mutual admiration rather than a trial, or perhaps even a duel, to which Hepp had resorted on at least two previous occasions.[3]

Interestingly, I found no evidence that Hepp made any similar accusations to Zola after the publication of *Fécondité*, even though Zola's novel repeats the themes of *Another's Milk* to a much greater extent than Brieux's play. However, any attentive scholar of French literature could have told Hepp that he was far from the first man of letters to write about mercenary versus maternal breast-feeding.

In 1898, Dr. Gustave-Joseph Witkowski, a practicing physician in Paris and author of numerous books and articles popularizing medical knowledge, published an extensive list of representations of breast-feeding throughout history under the titillating title *Tétoniana: Medical, Literary and Artistic Curiosities on Breasts and Breast-Feeding*. Witkowski cites, in no particular order and with little overall organization, examples from around the world and various time periods in the categories of medicine, art, and literature, complete with illustrations. In the last category, he mentions Hepp's *Another's Milk*, calling it an exaggerated story of the dangers of wet-nursing (1898, 280). Witkowski's book, nicknamed by a colleague "the great dictionary of boobs" ("Le grand Larousse des tétons!"), offers ample evidence that the literary subject of breasts and breast-feeding existed long before Hepp penned his novel, even though the most prominent example in nineteenth-century literature would not be published until the following year (1898, 352).

In this book, I have shown the evolution of literary representations of breast-feeding from around the French Revolution to the dawn of the twentieth century. As we have seen, the subject enjoyed huge popularity after the publication of Rousseau's *Émile*, then waned during the first decades of the new century only to return with renewed energy toward the latter half of the 1800s. The eighteenth-century trend of literature as propaganda to promote maternal breast-feeding, seen in both literature and art of the Enlightenment and the Revolutionary period, became even more urgent during the Third Republic, with fears of France's depopulation following the Franco-Prussian War playing into the hands of those who wished simultaneously to glorify the Mother and keep women out of the public sphere. By promoting the symbol of Marianne as the breast-feeding personification of the Republic, pro-natalists such as Zola used the tried-and-true methods of Rousseau in an effort to control women's bodies for the good of the nation.

We have seen that the substantial literary, artistic, and medical propaganda campaign promoted by Rousseau and others in the late 1700s ultimately failed to convince French women to nurse their own children, and the same can be said of the pronatalist movement in the last years of the nineteenth century. While the wet-nursing industry experienced a slow and inevitable decline during this period, disappearing almost entirely by the end of the Great War in 1918, this change in social mores seemed to result from the increasing availability and affordability of pasteurized milk, rather than an upsurge in maternal breast-feeding (Fay-Sallois, 1980, 248). As clinics in Paris and elsewhere began to distribute pasteurized milk free of charge or at reduced cost, women finally had a safe and viable alternative to breast-feeding that did not involve entrusting their children to other women poorer than themselves. Even the fictional Dr. Boutan, Zola's medical spokesperson in *Fécondité*, conceded that "when the mother absolutely cannot fulfill her duty, there is the bottle, which, if it is well kept, used carefully, with sterilized milk, produces satisfactory results" (n.d., 387).[4] The name of Zola's fictional doctor is reminiscent of that of well-known obstetrician Dr. Pierre Budin, founder of the *consultation des nourrisons* (nurslings' consultation service) at La Charité hospital in Paris in 1892 and inventor of the *Galactophore* baby bottle (Rothschild, 1899, 60–61).

The rise of safe bottle-feeding finally accomplished what centuries of medical, moralist, and literary persuasion could not: the emancipation of the maternal breast. As George Sussman points out, with sterilized milk becoming more readily available and more affordable than hiring a wet nurse, mothers now had the option to feed their infants without sacrificing either their bodily autonomy or their child's health (1982, 184). Zola's turn-of-the-century utopian vision of a future in which mothers' milk flowed in a continuum with the life forces of Mother Earth, "the flood of eternal life for the eternal harvest of beings" (n.d., 346), was already becoming obsolete even as it was written, forced to give way to new technologies such as pasteurization and ultimately to new ways of conceiving and organizing the family, the world, and the French nation. Never again would the image of the breast-feeding woman hold the power and prominence in French literature and in French authors' imaginations that we have observed throughout the nineteenth century.

In the social upheavals of the twentieth century, Marianne's exposed breasts became less maternal and more overtly sexual, modeled after movie star and sex symbol Brigitte Bardot in 1969 and many others since (Agulhon and Bonté, 1992, 92–94). No longer useful as either a tool of governmental propaganda or a phantasm for male authors deprived of their own mothers' attention, the breast-feeding maternal figures that populated nineteenth-century French fiction receded into literary history, along with the hordes of wet nurses that used to populate Parisian parks on a Sunday afternoon and the *meneuses* who crowded trains to and from the Morvan with packets of newborns under their arms. We can imagine Rousseau's disappointment at the failure of maternal breast-feeding to triumph over all obstacles, but it seems fitting to give George Sand the final word: "[Rousseau] created nursing women (*nourrices*) when he believed he was creating mothers. He mistook the maternal breast for the creating soul (*l'âme géneratrice*)" (Sand, 1861, 33).[5] As Sand foretold, twentieth-century women discovered the power to nurture their children without nursing them, and that made all the difference.

Notes

Chapter 1: Nursing Mothers in Eighteenth-Century France: The Personal is Political

1   "Celle qui nourrit l'enfant d'un autre au lieu du sien est une mauvaise mère; comment sera-t-elle une bonne nourrice? [...] Mais que les mères daignent nourrir leurs enfants, les mœurs vont se réformer d'elles-mêmes, les sentiments de la nature se réveiller dans tous les cœurs; l'Etat va se repeupler." (All translations are my own, unless otherwise indicated.)

2   "[A]u-dessus des autres hommes"; "un modèle de toutes les vertus." From a letter from Mme de Polignac to Mme de Verdelin in 1760. Quoted in Guéhenno, 1952, 69.

3   "Ah! s'il a voulu les priver de quelques droits étrangers à leur sexe, comme il leur a rendu tous ceux qui lui appartiennent à jamais! [...] s'il les a fait descendre d'un trône usurpé, comme il les a replacées sur celui que la nature leur a destiné!"

4   "C'est l'éloquence de Rousseau qui ranima le sentiment maternel, dans une certaine classe de la société; il fit connaître aux mères ce devoir et ce bonheur; il leur inspira le désir de ne céder à personne les premières caresses de leurs enfans."

5   "[N]e leur a-t-il pas appris à retrouver dans leur enfant une seconde jeunesse, dont l'espérance recommence pour elles, quand la première s'évanouit"? Ah! tout n'est pas encore perdu pour la mère malheureuse dont les fautes ou la destinée ont empoisonné la vie!"

6   See the paintings, *Jeune femme allaitant son enfant* (Louis-Roland Trinquesse, 1777, oil on canvas) and *Mère allaitant son enfant* (Jean-Laurent Mosnier, 1782, oil on canvas), both featured in the exhibition catalogue, Kayser, 2003.

7   "Je fus bientôt rétablie parce que je nourrissais, et d'ailleurs j'étais contente, heureuse, bien soignée, et je recevais sans cesse des marques d'attention de M. d'Ermancour."

8   "Prenons garde pourtant de nous laisser tromper par ces jolis tableaux
de ménage, inspirés bien plutôt par les aspirations que par les mœurs du
temps."

9   "Cette capitale se trouve tous les jours dépeuplée d'un nombre infini
d'enfans, que l'on envoie à quinze, vingt, trente lieues aux environs, & dont
certainement il n'en revient pas une vingtième partie à la maison paternelle;
un Auteur Anglois a fait cette remarque il y a long-temps." ["This capital
is each day depopulated by an infinite number of children sent to fifteen,
twenty, thirty *lieues* out of the city, of which certainly not even a twentieth
part return to their paternal home; an English author noticed this long ago."]
The English author to whom Deleurye refers is Haris in *Maladie des enfans,*
par Haris, premier médecin du Roi d'Angleterre, translated into French in
1705 by Devaux.

10   "Quels sont les avantages, dans l'ordre physique, moral et politique, de
l'allaitement des enfans par leurs mères?"

11   "Mille écrits retentissent de l'utilité & des avantages sans nombre de
l'allaitement des enfans par leurs mères. [...] Il est des vérités qu'il faut
répéter souvent: pour les faire goûter, pour les faire sentir, il faut les dire
pendant des siècles, il faut les dire tous les jours."

12   "Elle voulut le nourrir elle-même, bien entendu; c'était encore un peu
excentrique, mais elle était de celles qui avaient lu l'Emile avec religion
et qui voulaient donner le bon exemple. En outre, elle avait le sentiment
maternel extrêmement [56] développé, et ce fut, chez elle, une passion qui
lui tint lieu de toutes les autres. Mais la nature se refusa à son zèle. Elle
n'eut pas de lait, et pendant quelques jours, qu'en dépit des plus atroces
souffrances elle s'obstina à faire téter son enfant, elle ne put le nourrir que
de son sang. Il fallut y renoncer; ce fut pour elle une violente douleur et
comme un sinistre pronostique."

13   "Mme d'Eu est accouchée hier à midi d'une fille . . . Je suis sortie ce
matin pour les aller voir [...] Bon Dieu! combien une nouvelle accouchée
qu'on trouve seule, sans enfant, me paraît bizarre! La pauvre enfant suçait
ses doigts et buvait du lait de vache, dans une chambre éloignée de sa mère,
en attendant la mercenaire qui devait l'allaiter. Le père était fort pressé de
faire faire la cérémonie du baptême, pour expédier au village cette petite
créature. Tiens, mon ami, ce n'est pas ma faute; mais je les estime tous les
deux encore un peu moins depuis que j'ai été témoin de leur indifférence."

14   "Nous passâmes quatre années à Amiens; j'y fus mère et nourrice, sans
cesser de partager le travail de mon mari."

15   "Les mères de Paris ne nourrissent pas leurs enfans, et nous osons dire
qu'elles font bien. Ce n'est point dans l'air épais et fétide de la capitale, ce
n'est point au milieu du tumulte des affaires, ce n'est point au milieu de
la vie trop active ou trop dissipée qu'on y mène, que l'on peut accomplir

tous les devoirs de la maternité. Il faut la campagne, il faut une vie égale et champêtre, pour ne point se détruire en donnant son lait à ses enfans."

16   "[L]e modèle d'une direction éclairée, active, vigilante."

17   "Chargé d'un enfant de plus, le petit bourgeois n'en boit pas moins, tandis que le nouveau-né, remis entre les mains d'une nourrice, part pour la campagne. Le père et la mère ne le reverront que dans deux ans; et l'enfant fuyant alors leurs embrassemens, se rejetera sur le sein de la paysanne dont il aura sucé le lait. […] Avec des nourrices, des gouvernantes, des précepteurs, des colleges et des couvens, certaines femmes ne s'apperçoivent presque pas qu'elles sont meres."

18   See Étienne Aubry's *Adieux à la nourrice*, 1776, oil on canvas, at the Clark Institute, or Greuze's *Retour de nourrice*, drawing, 1760s.

19   "Un enfant amené par sa nourrice à sa mère, qu'il ne veut pas reconnaître."

20   "Peut-être aussi aura-t-il affermi le courage de quelque jeune épouse. […] Puisse-t-elle céder aux conseils donnés par ce tableau que de larmes elle s'épargnera! Ce doit être un cruel supplice pour une mère, que de voir son enfant donner, dès le berceau, un démenti à la nature."

21   "Tous les enfans qui y naissent [à Paris] vont en nourrice, la moitié meurent, et les registres mortuaires des paroisses de la ville ne sont pas chargés de leurs noms; il ne faut donc plus compter par le registre des baptêmes, ni par celui des morts."

22   "[P]ourquoi ne pas parler d'un spectacle du moins consolant et qui frappe incessamment nos regards? C'est celui que nous offre une multitude d'enfants allaités par leurs mères. […] Jamais dans aucune ville, dans aucun temps de ma vie, un pareil nombre d'enfants n'avait frappé mes regards. La maternité devient pour nos Françaises un degré de plus d'agrément; toutes nourrissent, toutes s'honorent d'être mères et toutes sentent que la seule et bonne nourrice est la véritable mère. La maternité est tellement en honneur, que ses fonctions font taire tous les propos oisifs qu'inventaient la malice et la médisance. Le sexe est justifié de toutes ses faiblesses, dès qu'il offre une nourrice soigneuse et attentive."

23   "Les pages immortelles qu'écrivit Rousseau sur le même sujet, inspirèrent un tel enthousiasme, que la plupart des mères de son temps voulurent, à l'envi, nourrir elles-mêmes leurs enfans. La coutume en devint bientôt presque universelle, même dans les plus hautes conditions. Mais en France, tout généralement n'est qu'éphémère […] Il n'y est donc plus de mode aujourd'hui que les mères donnent à leurs enfans la nourriture qui seule néanmoins leur convienne."

24   "Vous, nourrir votre enfant? J'en ai pensé mourir de rire. Quand bien même vous seriez assez forte pour cela, croyez-vous que je consentisse à un semblable ridicule?"

25   "Ma chère amie, quel que puisse être l'avis de Messieurs les Accoucheurs et Médecins, perdez ce projet de vue absolument. Il n'y a pas le sens commun. Quel diable de satisfaction peut-on trouver à nourrir un enfant?"

26   "La nature nous imposa sans doute la douce obligation d' allaiter nos enfans, et nous ne pouvons nous en dispenser que lorsque nous y sommes forcées par d' autres devoirs plus essentiels encore."

27   "[L]e coït trop fréquent des nourrices."

28   "Je ne dirai point avec les pères de l'Eglise, que toute mère qui refuse d'alaiter [*sic*] son enfant, est une marâtre barbare."

29   "[S]'il se trouve dans le péril de l'incontinence, la femme doit, si elle le peut, mettre son enfant en nourrice afin de pourvoir à l'infirmité de son mari." Quoted in Knibiehler and Fouquet, 1980, 93.

30   "Parce qu'ils n'acceptaient ni la contraception ni l'infidélité conjugale, les théologiens catholiques avaient trouvé dans la mise en nourrice la solution de l'incompatibilité des fonctions de nourrice et d'épouse."

31   Artificial feeding, while not uncommon in this period, almost always resulted in disastrous mortality rates. This remained true until Pasteur's method of sterilizing cow's milk became accessible and affordable in the early twentieth century.

32   "On doibt avoir soing au regime de la nourriçe, soit au manger & boire, dormir & veiller, exercice, & repos, & les diversifier selon la disposition & habitude de l'enfant: [...] elle evitera toutes viandes qui eschauffent le sang, comme espisseries, patisseries, saleures, moutarde, vins forts, & sans eau, & surtout aussi la colere, & toutes choses qui brulent le sang."

33   "[L]es jeunes femmes, dont les mères n'ont pas nourri, privées des conseils & des exemples domestiques, ignorent mille choses qui, dans le détail, paroissent peu importantes, mais dont l'ensemble contribue beaucoup au succès de la nourriture."

34   "Le peu de progrès qu'a fait la nourriture naturelle depuis ce tems-là prouve bien [...] qu'on ne profite pas toujours, autant qu'on le pourroit, de la peine que prennent les gens éclairés & humains de faire part aux autres du fruit de leurs méditations & de leur expérience."

35   "Je vois avec une grande satisfaction, que le nombre des femmes qui nourrissent leurs propres enfans augmente chaque jour." ["I see with great satisfaction that the number of women who breast-feed their own children is growing each day."] Le Rebours, 1775, iii.

36   "[A] pour objet de rappeler aux Mères, que le soin de nourrir elles-mêmes leurs Enfans, est le plus sacré de tous les devoirs."

37   "[L]'unique but que je me propose est de déterminer quelles sont les mères qui ne doivent point allaiter."

38   "La grossesse d'ensuite j'ai résolu de braver toutes les oppositions, le saint secret que j'ai trouvé pour y parvenir a été de faire mon coup à la

sourdine. La crainte d'inquiéter mon mari sur ma santé, celle de me brouiller avec mes parents, de négliger le talent de la peinture que j'ai, l'exemple de plusieurs femmes de ma connoissance qui, au lieu de réussir à nourrir, ont été obligée [*sic*] de renoncer après avoir souffert beaucoup, l'embaras de trois petits enfants à la fois chez moi et peu de secours, toutes ces difficultés ne m'ont point arrêtée."

39   "[M]on premier & principal objet a été d'épargner aux femmes, qui sont dans l'intention de nourrir, les douleurs & les embarras que plusieurs d'entre elles pourroient essuyer faute de sçavoir par elles-mêmes ce qu'il faut faire."

40   "[J]e ne connois pas d'ouvrage qui puisse faire autant de bien; & il en fera d'autant plus qu'étant l'ouvrage d'une femme respectable, qui ne dit que ce qu'elle a fait & ce qu'elle a vu, on lui donnera une confiance qu'on a rarement pour les ouvrages des Médecins."

41   "[F]ait par une dame qui en a eu un très-grand nombre qu'elle a tous élevés elle-même, et dont aucun n'est mort; et qui, par son industrie, ses réflexions et sa longue expérience, a su mettre l'Art d'élever les enfans à la portée de toutes les mères, de quelque condition, état ou profession qu'elles soient, en en rendant la pratique d'une aisance singulière."

42   "[Q]u'il est à souhaiter que cet Ouvrage se répande de plus en plus dans le Public, & que toutes les mères s'y conforment exactement."

43   "Je n'ai pas la sçience des Médecins, mais j'ai l'expérience pratique."

44   "Je ne dis que les choses dont je suis sûre. Si l'on veut se gouverner exactement d'après mon plan, on sera certain du succès."

45   "Il me reste à tracer le plan de la conduite qu'il faut suivre pour réussir dans l'allaitement. Je ne crois pas pouvoir prendre en cela un meilleur guide que Madame Le Rebours, que l'expérience, une judiciaire exercée & des connoissances au-dessus de celles qui sont communes aux personnes de son sexe, ont mis en état d'instruire les femmes qui veulent s'acquitter des devoirs de mère."

46   "Madame Le Rebours, qui, par son *Avis aux mères*, s'est placée au rang des partisans les plus éclairés de l'allaitement maternel."

47   "Quelques-uns de ces ouvrages n'ont pas été inutiles à l'époque où ils ont paru, pour combattre des usages évidemment contraires au bien-être et aux intérêts des enfans; mais aucun n'établit de règles d'après l'observation des faits et les notions de la science."

48   "[D]ans un ouvrage destiné à servir de guide aux jeunes mères, il y a toute une série de questions spéciales qui ne peuvent être complètement traitées sans la collaboration d'un médecin."

49   "[L]'allaitement doit être réglé de manière que l'enfant prenne ses repas à des heures à-peu-près fixes […] et non pas sans ordre et à toute heure." ["Breast-feeding should be regulated so that the child takes his meals more

or less at regular intervals […] and not in a disorderly fashion at any and all hours of the day."]

50 "Tout enfant qui ne gagne 15 à 20 grammes tous les jours doit être envisagé comme *mal nourri* ou *malade*. […] *Il est alors du devoir de la nourrice de consulter un médecin et de faire examiner son lait*." ["Any child who does not gain 15 to 20 grams each day must be considered *malnourished* or *ill*. […] *It is then the nursing mother's duty to consult a doctor and to have her milk examined*."] (Author's emphasis.)

51 "[N]'a cessé d'opposer aux diktats des professionnels de santé l'expérience vécue des mères: importance de la tétée précoce, tétées à la demande, sans minutage ni intervalle à respecter, tétées nocturnes […] respect des besoins de l'enfant (regarder le bébé plutôt que la pendule ou la balance) […] tout le contraire de ce que préconisaient à l'époque les professionnels et les manuels."

52 "[Q]ue ces eaux fécondes qui jaillissent de tes mamelles, que cette boisson pure qui abreuva les premiers Humains, consacrent dans cette coupe de la fraternité et de l'égalité, les sermens que te fait la France en ce jour!" "Que toutes les vertus guerrières et généreuses coulent, avec le lait maternel, dans le cœur de tous les nourrissons de la France!" For more on the similarities between Zola's Marianne and Republican rhetoric, see Mayer-Robin, 2000, 69–80.

53 "Ah! pourquoi, lorsque la maternité offre tant de douceurs, existe-t-il des êtres assez dénaturés pour en oublier les premiers devoirs et en méconnoître les charmes? Comment a-t-on vu des mères ordonner qu'on arrachât à leur vue l'innocente créature qu'elles venoient de mettre au monde! heureusement ces monstres sont rares sur la terre! heureusement les lois sont-là pour venger la Nature!"

54 "[P]uisse bientôt arriver [le jour] […] où vous pourrez librement déchirer le voile que vous avez jeté sur la nature."

55 "Il sera créé et organisé un établissement général de Secours publics, pour élever les enfants abandonnés, soulager les pauvres infirmes, et fournir du travail aux pauvres valides qui n'auraient pu s'en procurer."

56 "Ceux qui se présenteront pour réclamer, au nom de l'enfant qui va naître, des secours qui leur sont dus, seront tenus de se soumettre à faire allaiter l'enfant par sa mère." The decree guarantees 18 *livres* to mothers of newborns, plus 12 additional *livres* to mothers who nurse their own infants.

57 "Toute fille qui déclarera vouloir allaiter elle-même l'enfant dont elle sera enceinte, et qui aura besoin des secours de la nation, aura droit de les réclamer."

Chapter 2: The Absence of the Breast in the Tale of the Romantic Hero

1   "Raconterons-nous la tendresse de l'ours, qui, semblable à la femme sauvage, pousse l'amour maternel jusqu' à allaiter ses enfans après leur mort?"
2   "Celle qui a eu le plus d'enfants."
3   "[M]achine à enfanter," "le moule des braves."
4   "'A quand le vingt-cinquième?' [...] 'Je suis aux ordres de Votre Majesté.'"
5   "Bah! Une nuit de Paris compensera tout cela."
6   "Cet objectif réaliste élimine toute idéalisation, toute exaltation de la maternité. Sur ce point, Napoléon régresse par rapport à Rousseau ou à la Convention."
7   "[A] moins d'impossibilité absolue, dûment constatée."
8   "[C]es mères prendront l'engagement de nourrir elles-mêmes, ou d'élever au lait leurs enfans, si pour quelques causes extraordinaires elles ne pouvaient pas nourrir."
9   See Jean-Auguste-Dominique Ingres' paintings, *Portrait of Napoleon as First Consul*, 1804 (Musée des Beaux-Arts de Liège, Belgium) and *Napoleon on his Imperial Throne*, 1806 (Musée de l'Armée, Hôtel des Invalides, Paris).
10   "[N]os grand'mères et mères [le] savaient par cœur."
11   S'éveille-t-il? son sein, à l'instant présenté, / Dans les flots d'un lait pur lui verse la santé. / Qu'importe la fatigue à sa tendresse extrême? / Elle vit dans son fils, et non plus dans soi-même; / Et se montre, aux regards d'un époux éperdu, / Belle de son enfant à son sein suspendu. / Oui, ce fruit de l'hymen, ce trésor d'une mère, / Même à ses propres yeux, est sa beauté première.
12   "Tombe aux pieds de ce sexe à qui tu dois ta mère!"
13   "[C]e sexe à qui je dois [...] beaucoup moins que je ne lui ai donné."
14   "Lorsque j'ai composé ce poème [...] j'ai [...] voulu, en retraçant [les] avantages [des femmes], ramener dans leur société un peuple valeureux que les secousses de la révolution ont accoutumé à s'en éloigner, et et, par ce moyen, le rappeler à sa première urbanité, qu'il a presque perdue dans la lutte des partis. Avouons-le, les Français avoient les grâces d'Athènes, ils ont pris un peu de la rudesse de Sparte; et l'exemple de ceux de nos parvenus dont l'esprit a été foiblement cultivé, l'influence de cette génération nouvelle dont la guerre a interrompu ou altéré l'éducation, peuvent augmenter de jour en jour ce changement dans la physionomie nationale. [...] Eh! Si les chefs de la Terreur [...] avoient mieux appréciées [les femmes], ils auroient versé moins de sang; l'homme qui les chérit est rarement un barbare."
15   "Au nom de la pudeur, couvrez-moi le sein."
16   "L'enfant naît, la mamelle est pleine; la bouche du jeune convive n'est

point armée, de peur de blesser la coupe du banquet maternel: il croît; le lait devient plus nourrissant: on le sèvre; la merveilleuse fontaine tarit."

17   "Cette femme si foible, a tout-à-coup acquis des forces qui lui font surmonter des fatigues, que ne pourroit supporter l'homme le plus robuste."

18   "D'où lui vient cette adresse qu' elle n' avoit jamais eue? [...] Ses soins semblent être le fruit de l'expérience de toute sa vie; et cependant c'est-là son premier-né!"

19   "Il n'y a pas de jour où, rêvant à ce que j'ai été, je ne revoie en pensée le rocher sur lequel je suis né, la chambre où ma mère m'infligea la vie [...] En sortant du sein de ma mère, je subis mon premier exil. [...] Que ne me laissait-on mourir?"

20   "[M]ère divine … partageant les sollicitudes de la mère terrestre."

21   "Ma mère d'ailleurs, pleine d'esprit et de vertu, était préoccupée par les soins de la société et les devoirs de la religion. [...] Elle aimait la politique, le bruit, le monde."

22   "[A]bandonné aux mains des gens."

23   "Oh! Il faut que je me hâte de t'aller rejoindre, pour te chanter des chansons, et te présenter mon sein."

24   "Elle arrosa la terre de son lait; ensuite s'asseyant sur le gazon humide, elle parla à son enfant d'une voix attendrie; elle disoit: 'pourquoi te pleurois-je dans ton berceau de terre, ô mon nouveau-né! [...] Du moins tu as ignoré les pleurs; du moins ton cœur n'a point été exposé au souffle dévorant des hommes. [...] Heureux ceux qui meurent au berceau, ils n'ont connu que les baisers et les souris d'une mère!'"

25   "La femme renouvelle ses douleurs chaque fois qu'elle est mère, et elle se marie en pleurant. Que de maux dans la seule perte d' un nouveau-né, à qui l' on donnoit le lait, et qui meurt sur votre sein!"

26   "[C]omme mon lait étoit mauvais, à cause de la douleur, il a empoisonné mon enfant."

27   "Pauvre femme! Son lait à sa tête est monté."

28   "[E]lle ne pleura pas. Le lait avec la fièvre / soudain troubla sa tête et fit trembler sa lèvre."

29   "Dieu clément! À quoi sert / le regard maternel sans l'enfant qui repose? / À quoi bon ce sein blanc sans cette bouche rose?"

30   "Seigneur! Vous avez mis partout un noir mystère, / dans l'homme et dans l'amour, dans l'arbre et dans l'oiseau, / et jusque dans ce lait que réclame un berceau, / ambroisie et poison, doux miel, liqueur amère, / fait pour nourrir l'enfant ou pour tuer la mère!"

31   "Elle se renversait sur sa chaise en arrière, / Son fichu laissant voir son sein gonflé de lait, Et souriait au faible enfant, et l'appelait / Ange, trésor, amour; et mille folles choses. / Oh! comme elle baisait ces beaux petits pieds roses!"

32   "Elle ne mangeait pas; sa vie était sa fièvre; / Elle ne répondait à personne; sa lèvre / Tremblait."

33   "[E]lle se sentit mère une seconde fois."

34   "C'est moi. Ne le dis pas."

35   "Mères en deuil, vos cris là-haut sont entendus. / Dieu, qui tient dans sa main tous les oiseaux perdus, / Parfois au même nid rend la même colombe. / O mères! le berceau communique à la tombe."

36   "Je vous dirai peut-être quelque jour / Quel lait pur, que de soins, que de vœux, que d'amour, / Prodigués pour ma vie en naissant condamnée, / M'ont fait deux fois l'enfant de ma mère obstinée [...] Ô l'amour d'une mère! amour que nul n'oublie! / Pain merveilleux qu'un dieu partage et multiplie!"

37   "J'ai tété ma mère qui a été ma nourrice; j'ai bu ton âme sur tes lèvres, et tu as été ma nourrice aussi, car tu m'as rempli d'idéal."

38   "Mon père, par une exception dont il ignora la cause, fut séparé du reste de la famille et enfermé dans la prison de Mâcon. Ma mère, qui me nourrissait alors, fut laissée seule dans l'hôtel de mon grand-père, sous la surveillance de quelques soldats de l'armée révolutionnaire. Et l'on s'étonne que les hommes dont la vie date de [37] ces jours sinistres aient apporté, en naissant, un goût de tristesse et une empreinte de mélancolie dans le génie français? Virgile, Cicéron, Tibulle, Horace lui-même, qui imprimèrent ce caractère au génie romain, n'étaient-ils pas nés, comme nous, pendant les grandes guerres civiles de Rome et au bruit des proscriptions de Marius, de Sylla, de César? Que l'on songe aux impressions de terreur ou de pitié qui agitèrent les flancs des femmes romaines pendant qu'elles portaient ces hommes dans leur sein! Que l'on songe au lait aigri de larmes que je reçus moi-même de ma mère pendant que la famille entière était dans une captivité qui ne s'ouvrait que pour la mort!"

39   "Ma pauvre mère m'apportait tous les jours dans ses bras au grenier, me montrait à mon père, m'allaitait devant lui, me faisait tendre mes petites mains vers les grilles de la prison; puis, me pressant le front contre sa poitrine, elle me dévorait de baisers, adressant ainsi au prisonnier toutes les caresses dont elle me couvrait à son intention."

40   "L'aimer, mais pour l'aimer étais-je un autre qu'elle? / N'étais-je pas nourri du suc de sa mamelle, / éclos de son amour, réchauffé dans son flanc, / la moelle de ses os, le plus pur de son sang? L'air qu'elle respirait dans sa chaste poitrine / ne fut-il pas neuf mois celui de ma narine? / De son cœur près du mien le moindre battement / ne m'inspirait-il pas le même sentiment? / Mon corps n'était-il pas tout son corps, et mon âme / un foyer emprunté qu'allume une autre flamme?"

41   "[L]es autres mères ne portent que neuf mois leur enfant dans leur sein; je puis dire que la mienne m'a porté douze ans dans le sien, et que

j'ai vécu de sa vie morale comme j'avais vécu de sa vie physique dans ses flancs, jusqu'au moment où j'en fus arraché pour aller vivre de la vie putride ou tout au moins glaciale des collèges."

42 "Une mère nourrice présentant son sein à son enfant, que lui amène une gouvernante." Salon of 1804. Currently in Musée Fragonard in Grasse, France, with the title: "Les Premiers Pas, ou la Mère nourrice."

43 "Un enfant amené par sa nourrice à sa mère, qu'il ne veut pas reconnaître." Location unknown.

44 "Peut-être aussi aura-t-il affermi le courage de quelque jeune épouse . . . Puisse-t-elle céder aux conseils donnés par ce tableau que de larmes elle s'épargnera! Ce doit être un cruel supplice pour une mère, que de voir son enfant donner, dès le berceau, un démenti à la nature."

45 "Un enfant que l'on ramène de nourrice, et qui se refuse aux embrassements de sa mère." Later called "Retour de nourrice." Musée-Château de Dieppe.

46 "Une jeune femme. N'ayant pu continuer à allaiter son enfant, elle le regarde téter la chèvre qui la supplée et s'abandonne aux réflexions que sa situation fait naître."

47 "Hélas, mon enfant, malgré ce joli sein que je te montre, la nature m'a refusé le bien de pouvoir te nourrir! Que j'envie le bonheur de cette chèvre. Je suis dans une étable, il est vrai, mais j'y suis avec mon enfant."

48 "Une jeune femme ayant perdu son enfant, lui a élevé un tombeau dans une vallée solitaire. Une pierre couverte de mousse et de gazon, et surmontée d'une croix où pend une couronne de roses, forme le modeste monument de l'amour maternel. La mère infortunée contemple avec une expression douleureuse et les yeux baignés de larmes le lieu qui renferme les restes d'un objet chéri."

49 "Ma mère n'avait jamais lu Jean-Jacques Rousseau et n'en avait peut-être pas beaucoup entendu parler, ce qui ne l'empêcha pas d'être ma nourrice, comme elle l'avait été et comme elle le fut de tous ses autres enfants."

50 "Je fus la nourrice de mon fils, comme plus tard je fus la nourrice de sa sœur."

51 "Bah! notre maître, je ne vois pas pourquoi nous allons dépenser cent quatre-vingts ou deux cents livres par an, comme si nous étions des messieurs et dames, et comme si j'étais hors d'âge pour nourrir mes enfants. J'ai plus de lait qu'il n'en faut pour cela. Ils ont déjà un mois, nos garçons, et voyez s'ils ne sont pas en bon état! La Merlaude que vous voulez donner pour nourrice à un des deux n'est pas moitié si forte et si saine que moi; son lait a déjà dix-huit mois, et ce n'est pas ce qu'il faut à un enfant si jeune."

52 "[S]ans se plaindre et sans souffrir."

53 "L'enfant fut le seul qui ne souffrit pas trop de cette détresse. Sa mère avait peu de lait; mais la voisine partageait avec le nourrisson celui de son déjeuner, et chaque jour elle allait le promener dans ses bras au soleil du

quai aux Fleurs. Il n'en faut pas davantage à un enfant de Paris pour croître comme une plante frêle, mais tenace."

54 "Mes enfants n'ont pas eu d'autre nourrice que moi, et les deux premiers ont souvent pressé mon sein dans la coulisse, entre deux scènes. Je me souviens qu'une fois le public me rappelait avec tant de despotisme après la première pièce, que j'ai été forcée de venir le saluer avec mon enfant sous mon châle."

55 "Ton petit ange Maurice a bien dormi cette nuit, bien tété ce matin, bien fait pipi et caca, etc."

56 "Il n'a pas compris les femmes, ce sublime Rousseau. [...] Il a fait des nourrices croyant faire des mères. Il a pris le sein maternel pour l'âme génératrice. Le plus spiritualiste des philosophes du siècle dernier a été matérialiste sur la question des femmes."

57 "La femme est donnée à l'homme pour qu'elle lui fasse des enfants. Elle est donc sa propriété comme l'arbre fruitier est celle du jardinier."

58 "[F]ort gras, peu velu, [il] a la peau blanche et présente un certain embonpoint qui n'est pas de notre sexe, ce qu'il observe parfois gaiement."

Chapter 3: Realism, Naturalism, and the Eroticization of Breast-Feeding

1 "Maria avait un enfant; c'était une petite fille [...] Maria l'allaitait elle-même et, un jour, je la vis découvrir sa gorge et lui présenter le sein. C'était une gorge grasse et ronde, avec une peau brune et des veines d'azur que l'on voyait dans cette chair ardente. Jamais je n'avais vue de femme nue alors. Oh! La singulière extase où me plongea la vue de ce sein; comme je le dévorai des yeux, comme j'aurais voulu seulement toucher cette poitrine! Il me semblait que si j'eusse posé mes lèvres, mes dents l'auraient mordue de rage et mon cœur se fondait en délices en pensant aux voluptés que donnerait ce baiser. Oh! Comme je l'ai revue souvent cette gorge palpitante."

2 "[U]n éclatant démenti donné aux théories nouvelles sur l'indépendance de la femme, et un ouvrage écrit dans un but essentiellement moral." *La Presse* (November 10, 1841). Cited in Andréoli, 1987, 257.

3 "[D]'une vie dépouillée de toute ferveur et de toute passion."

4 "A Louise l'orgasmique s'oppose Renée qui n'a jamais joui."

5 "[U]n substitut du plaisir" [...] "aussi riche sensuellement que celle dont se prévaut Louise."

6 "[D]es projections de fantasmes masculins."

7 "[M]ême si la femme est enfermée dans l'espace maternel créé par le discours masculin, l'expérience corporelle transgresse cet espace, et en même temps l'espace patriarcal."

8   "Le petit monstre a pris mon sein et a teté: voilà le *Fiat lux*! J'ai soudain été mère. [...] Ce petit être ne connaît absolument que notre sein. [...] Ses lèvres ont un amour inexprimable, et, quand elles s'y collent, elles y font à la fois une douleur et un plaisir, un plaisir qui va jusqu'à la douleur, ou une douleur qui finit par un plaisir; je ne saurais t'expliquer une sensation qui du sein rayonne en moi jusqu'aux sources de la vie, car il semble que ce soit un centre d'où partent mille rayons qui réjouissent le cœur et l'âme. Enfanter, ce n'est rien; mais nourrir, c'est enfanter à toute heure. Oh! Louise, il n'y a pas de caresses d'amant qui puissent valoir celles de ces petites mains roses qui se promènent si doucement, et cherchent à s'accrocher à la vie."

9   "[U]n roman *féminin* – un texte véritablement transsexuel, où un esprit parvient, non pas seulement à entrer dans le corps de l'autre [...] mais, ce qui est singulièrement plus difficile, à entrer dans le corps d'*une* autre." (Original emphasis.)

10   "Autant qu'il lui est possible, Balzac se met dans la peau d'une femme qui allaite et se fantasme avec des seins gonflés, inépuisables, sensuels, car là encore c'est bien d'une euphorie érotique qu'il s'agit. Si elle ne connait pas les mêmes ivresses que son amie Louise dans les bras de Macumer, Renée n'en tient pas moins à lui faire savoir qu'elle a accès à un autre mode de jouir, dont celle qui n'est qu'amante ne peut avoir idée."

11   "Transmigrate, *v.*" q.v. *Oxford English Dictionary* online. www.oed.com/. Accessed December 20, 2021.

12   Pierre Leroux (1797–1871), writer and philosopher of the French Romantic socialism movement, and lifelong friend of George Sand. Sand refers here to Leroux's beliefs on reincarnation. For more, see Lacassagne, 1973.

13   "[I]l faut, mon cher, que vous ayez, suivant nos idées de Leroux, un souvenir d'existence antérieure où vous auriez été femme et mère. Après tout vous savez tant de choses que personne ne sait."

14   "Balzac, dans un passage de *Mémoires de deux jeunes mariées*, étonne par la modernité de ses propos sur l'expérience de l'allaitement. Il se complaît à décrire les joies d'allaiter, joies physiques et psychiques mêlées. [...] On ne saurait mieux décrire ce plaisir de l'allaitement, pour le bébé comme pour la mère, plaisir qui, selon Balzac, fait la mère et rivalise avec le plaisir sexuel. Ce roman est écrit en 1841, rares seront les auteurs qui, dans la seconde moitié du siècle, se risqueront à célébrer l'allaitement avec autant de lyrisme."

15   "Renée mère, c'est Zulma. [...] Grâce aux confidences écrites et orales de Zulma Carraud, il a pu transposer sa propre sensibilité et décrire les joies et les douleurs de la maternité, comme aucun homme ne l'a sans doute jamais fait."

16   "Vous ne saurez jamais ce que c'est que d'être mère; ce privilège de maternité nous console de tous ceux qua la nature vous a donnés, sans doute comme dédommagement, et aussi de ceux, bien plus nombreux, que vous vous êtes arrogés."

17   "[M]on moi s'efface complètement dans l'existence de ce nouvel enfant." November 14, 1834.

18   "Trop incomplète pour avoir pu nourrir mes enfans, je les prends au sortir des bras de leur nourrice, et alors ils m'appartiennent."

19   "[J]e me plongeai dans ce dos comme un enfant qui se jette dans le sein de sa mère, et je baisai toutes ces épaules en y roulant ma tête."

20   "[I]l n'y a pas de caresses d'amant qui puissent valoir celles de ces petites mains roses."

21   "Le vieux grand-père devient enfant, je crois; il me regarde avec admiration. La première fois que je suis descendue à déjeuner, et qu'il m'a vue mangeant et donnant à teter à son petit-fils, il a pleuré. Cette larme dans ces deux yeux secs où il ne brille guère que des pensées d'argent m'a fait un bien inexprimable; il m'a semblé que le bonhomme comprenait mes joies."

22   "[Q]ui le premier lui a fait connaître de pareilles joies […] et lui a appris le grand art de la maternité?"

23   We will refer to the novel with its original French title, *Fécondité*, throughout. The only English translation called it *Fruitfulness,* but a better translation might be *Fertility* or *Fecundity.*

24   "C'était, plus haut et plus vrai que le culte de la vierge, le culte de la mère, la mère aimée et glorifiée, douloureuse et grande, dans la passion qu'elle souffre, pour l'éternelle floraison de la vie." All translations of *Fécondité* are my own.

25   See Chapter 1 for more on Revolutionary iconography on breast-feeding and Chapter 4 for more on the political symbolism in Zola's novel.

26   "Tu sais que, pendant les neuf mois de la grossesse et pendant les quinze mois de l'allaitement, nous ne pourrons même pas nous embrasser. Ça fait deux ans sans la moindre caresse […] N'est-ce pas, mon cher ami, qu'un mari raisonnable, qui a le souci de la bonne santé de la mère et de l'enfant ne touche plus à sa femme de tout ce temps-là?"

27   "C'est un peu exagéré. Mais, tout de même, il y a du vrai. Le mieux est en effet de s'abstenir.

– S'abstenir, tu entends, Claire? Hein! le vilain mot! Est-ce là ce que tu veux?"

28   "[E]lle sortit de la camisole l'un de ses petits seins durs de guerrière, que le lait gonflait maintenant, épanoui comme une grande fleur de vie, blanche et rose; tandis que l'enfant goulu, ne voyant pas encore, promenait les mains, tâtonnait des lèvres. Lorsqu'il eut trouvé, il téta violemment, buvant toute la mère, jusqu'au meilleur de son sang. […] Il revint, il s'oublia,

dans le ravissement du spectacle. […] Il n'était pas d'épanouissement plus glorieux, de symbole plus sacré de l'éternité vivante: l'enfant au sein de la mère. C'était l'enfantement qui continuait, la mère se donnait encore toute pendant de longs mois, achevait de créer l'homme, ouvrait la fontaine de sa vie qui coulait de sa chair sur le monde. Elle n'arrachait de ses entrailles l'enfant nu et fragile que pour le reprendre contre sa gorge tiède, nouveau refuge d'amour, où il se réchauffait, où il se nourrissait."

29   "Elle avait abaissé sur le petit ses beaux yeux tendres, elle le regardait téter goulûment, d'un regard d'immense amour, heureuse même du mal qu'il lui faisait parfois, ravie quand il la buvait trop fort, comme elle disait. Et elle continua d'une voix de rêve: "Mon enfant à une autre, oh! non, jamais, jamais! J'en serais trop jalouse, je veux qu'il ne soit fait que de moi, sorti de moi, achevé par moi. Ce ne serait plus mon enfant, si une autre l'achevait. […] Cher, cher enfant bien-aimé! quand il tète si fort, je sens que je passe toute en lui, c'est un délice.""

30   "[L]e sein blanc, d'une douceur de soie, dont le lait gonflait la pointe rose, telle que le bouton d'où naîtrait la fleur de vie. […] l'enfant, sur sa gorge ouverte et libre, tétait à longs flots le lait tiède, de même que ces verdures innombrables buvaient la vie de la terre."

31   "Un flot de sang réchauffa le cœur de Mathieu, lorsque, tout d'un coup, il eut la pensée de Marianne, saine et forte, qui devait l'attendre, sur le pont de l'Yeuse, dans la vaste campagne, avec leur petit Gervais au sein."

32   "[Q]ui se trouve ainsi lavée du péché original de la sexualité. Il semble donc que la femme ne puisse vraiment être acceptée qu'en tant que mère que l'enfant sanctifie."

33   "[L]'usage de mettre les enfans en nourrice, est une cause de dépopulation." For more on Le Rebours, see Chapter 1.

34   "[Q]uasi avec le lait les mœurs et les vices de la nourrice influent dans les enfans."

35   "Quel étrange abus est-ce donc de pervertir cette noblesse naturelle de l'homme qui nous vient de nature, de corrompre son corps et son esprit […] en lui faisant prendre la nourriture dégénérée d'un lait étranger et bâtard?"

36   "Ils en redoutent les conséquences possibles; immédiates: c'est l'altération du lait."

37   "[L]a jouissance altère la nature du lait, le prive de sa partie sucrée et détermine ainsi de graves accidents chez le nourrisson."

38   "[U]n lait corrompu sucé en nourrice."

39   "Tous les départements, sans exception, présentent une diminution de la natalité depuis le commencement du siècle."

40   "[N]ous persistons dans notre coupable indifférence et dans nos habitudes infanticides. Comme par le passé, la population des villes confie

ses enfants à des nourrices; celles-ci restent attachées à leur routine. Les nourrissons continuent à mourir."

41 "L'auteur semble n'avoir eu d'autre mérite (c'est la marque du génie) que d'écrire ce que nous avons à tout moment sous les yeux."

42 "[U]n moyen épouvantable qui amène fatalement des ennuis. Un enfant nourri par une étrangère puise sa vie dans un élément nouveau et peut en récolter les vices et les maladies."

43 "[L]e seul fait de choisir ce métier de nourrice les met, pour moi, au bas de l'échelle humaine. Il n'y a pas d'industrie plus révoltante, plus dégradante."

44 "Marianne [...] n'était point seule à nourrir, la sève d'avril gonflait les labours, agitait les bois d'un frisson, soulevait les herbes hautes où elle était noyée. Et, sous elle, du sein de la terre en continuel enfantement, elle sentait bien ce flot qui la gagnait, qui l'emplissait, qui lui redonnait du lait, à mesure que le lait ruisselait de sa gorge. Et c'était là le flot de lait coulant par le monde, le flot d'éternelle vie pour l'éternelle moisson des êtres."

45 See Chapter 1 for more on breast-feeding and revolution.

46 "[L]a maternité devient le rachat de la faute sexuelle, que seule la femme considérée comme une bonne mère peut être acceptée, alors que les autres sont présentées soit comme des personnages négatifs, soit comme des femmes fatales."

47 "[D]ans l'épanouissement de la femme qui suit la maternité, Zola ne distingue que le sein, ce sein dont la fonction nourricière justifie à ses yeux la fonction érotique."

48 "[N]auséabondes et malpropres, qui relèvent plutôt de la littérature médicale que du roman."

49 "[T]ableaux terribles, brossés avec une rare vigueur par un écrivain dont la pensée est singulièrement saine, sous ses audaces."

50 "Son roman, d'un symbolisme largement intelligible [...] convaincra [les jeunes mères] de la supériorité de l'allaitement maternel sur l'allaitement nourricier, et a fortiori sur l'alimentation au biberon. M. Hepp fera un tort énorme aux bureaux de nourrices; et qui l'en blâmera?"

51 "Bonne nourrice! Ah! Ah! Bonne nourrice! Voilà deux mots qui hurlent d'être accouplés! [...] Mais la connaissez-vous cette femme à qui vous allez confier votre enfant? Oubliez-vous que le moral de cette étrangère va opérer sur ce cerveau à l'état d'ébauche une suggestion de tous les instants qui peut retentir sur toute une vie?"

52 "[L]'histoire douloureusement vraie d'un enfant odieusement flétri par une de ces gueuses" (117).

53 For more on Brieux, see Conclusion.

54 "[D]es tas de journaux les ont publiés en feuilleton; ce ne sont point des ouvrages inconnus du public."

55 "[J]e le respecte, je l'admire et je le plains."

56 "[E]lle finit la ronde, jusque devant le cimetière on l'a eue, ils doivent être fatigués!"

57 "[Le] menton glabre, carré, et ses yeux impitoyables, profondément encaissés sous les sourcils blancs et revêches."

58 "Lentement elle vient, elle lui sourit, très fraîche. Et une curiosité l'aiguillonne, un besoin de savoir, de découvrir ce qui lui reste, à celui-là! Les jeunes, un vieux! Et elle s'avance plus près, passivement, avec une idée mauvaise d'être bonne, et de ses bras secs le vieux l'encercle, il la pétrit, il la broie; puis il se guette, pendant une seconde il attend, il espère, [52] éperdument, en son être mort. Oh c'est un moment d'horrible torture et sa face en pâlit. Rien – et pourtant le désir subsiste qui poigne, dévaste, la figure du vieux flageolant. Et la fille s'esclaffe."

59 "[A]avec la joie de lui fournir un plaisir."

60 "Alors, des griffes, il ouvre le caraco rose qui flotte sur ses chairs, plonge dans la chemise rugueuse, élargie, dont la coulisse de laine pend dénouée. Et longtemps ses doigts de vieux courent, ses lèvres bavent sur l'éblouissement de cette poitrine, et il contourne, il racle de sa langue les mamelles gonflées. Et la fille dit: – Tête donc, père Gérard, pour voir! Alors le vieux assure la pointe dans sa bouche flétrie, meut ses mâchoires édentées, et durcies et il reçoit le jet d'un lait pur."

61 "Assez, ça fait mal, il me boirait tout" [...] "courbé, tout barbouillé de blanc, suçant ses lèvres rentrées: et tandis qu'il la cherche encore, elle a déjà fui emportant sur elle la salive et le bleu des morsures de ce vieux."

62 "[A]h il ne s'est pas ennuyé, le père Gérard, d'avoir son sein et son lait pour rien! Cela se paye, à la Ville on la payera."

63 "Ce n'est pas à dire qu'ils ignoraient le récit de la femme romaine; mais ils auront été convaincus, et cela à juste titre, qu'au point de vue de l'art [...] pour l'effet psychologique à produire, un vieillard nourri par sa fille convenait le mieux."

64 "La grande vogue du thème, jusqu'au XIXe siècle, tient-elle à son riche contenu affectif et à son caractère incestueux?"

65 "[D]e bonnes, grasses et larges mamelles, [155] bien pleines de lait."

66 "Que crains-tu, homme de paix & de douceur? Ne suis-je pas ta fille? N'es-tu pas notre pere? Mon bien-aimé me l'a tant dit! Il donneroit pour toi son sang. Moi, je t'offre mon lait. Daigne puiser la vie dans ce sein que tu as fait tressaillir tant de fois, lorsqu'on me racontoit les prodiges de ta bonté."

67 "Elle est obscure dans ses intentions et trouble dans son message. Le ravissement qu'elle suscite est pervers."

68 "Elle adorait l'entendre crier, à sa manière de jadis, pour rentrer en sa possession, pour le calmer à elle seule, de son lait! Alors quand elle le

montrait assoupi, ainsi que par miracle, sur sa mamelle, elle le remerciait de lui rester fidèle, d'aimer son lait par-dessus tout." One might wonder if Freud read Hepp's novel before writing, in *Three Essays on Sexuality*: "No one who has seen a baby sinking back satiated from the breast and falling asleep with flushed cheeks and a blissful smile can escape the reflection that this picture persists as a prototype of the expression of sexual satisfaction in later life" (1989, 263). Freud certainly had read *Fécondité*, since he included it in his list of "ten good books," in response to a request by publisher Hugo Heller in 1906 (540).

69   "L'instinct pris avec la nourriture de l'autre faisait son œuvre. Le lait maudit de l'étrangère s'inoculait dans sa chair."

70   "[L]e venin de son lait est prospère [...] l'œuvre de sa destruction est définitive et scellé."

71   "Ah, monsieur ne sait pas! tous les enfants ont du lait, ils l'apportent en naissant, et il faut le leur chasser!"

72   "[L]a nourrice le triturait, le brassait aux mamelons."

73   "[L]a mère venait de frôler la mort pour s'être obstinée à le stériliser, ce lait sacré! et maintenant l'innocent à son tour pâtissait, et c'était cela qui lui valait sa première douleur? Geneviève, l'enfant, atteints par la même cause? Oh! c'était trop, et ce gémissement d'enfant auquel on ôte le lait de la mère [...] profondément retentit dans Michel."

74   "[L]e corps si blanc du petit, avec des lignes fermes et grasses, peu à peu de l'obscurité se détacha, il se dessinait, s'allongeait hardiment, et il la tentait. [...] au mignon sevré elle représenta le sein, il le prit, il le reconnut, il le retrouva avec une joie et il s'endormit. [...] Et le plaisir pour elle fut d'autant plus vivace qu'elle l'avait retardé; maintenant, régulièrement l'enfant recevait cette violente tendresse, et la fille de Sennelisse s'excusait à ses propres yeux, en se disant que cela lui venait du cœur."

75   "Alors courbé, effaré, Michel la découvrit aux seins, les draps volèrent, et en plein visage Michel reçut une éclaboussure de lait. C'était une fusée énorme, un jaillissement furieux des deux mamelles douloureuses, et d'un blanc formidablement veiné. Et ces veines semblaient craquer, se tordre, et ramper sur le gonflement des globes ainsi que des serpents. Et parfois aussi on eût dit un déchaînement de tempête sur la gorge; elle oscillait sous la formation, l'élan d'un jet qui allait sourdre; puis quand tout s'était élancé, par saccades puissantes, cela coulait encore, coulait toujours, se répandait aqueux, fluide, sans arrêt, partout, sur elle, et sur le lit. – Le lait! s'écria Geneviève, il monte, il monte, il monte! Et sous ce ruissellement qui sortait d'elle, l'inondait, avec par instant des impétuosités, des tourbillons de trombe, elle s'évanouissait, roulait, perdait l'âme."

76   "[L]e flot de semence détourné de sa juste emploi, tombé au pave où rien ne poussait."

77   "Entre 1760 et 1925, on a pu recenser en France une douzaine de volumes de vulgarisation médicale où la masturbation figure parmi les préoccupations majeures des hygiénistes."

78   "Songez donc! on ne trompe pas impunément un organe. [...] Toute fonction qui ne s'accomplit pas dans l'ordre normal devient un danger permanent de troubles."

79   "Toujours de nouvelles semences enfantaient des moissons nouvelles, le soleil toujours remontait de l'horizon, le lait ruisselait sans fin des gorges nourricières, sève éternelle de l'humanité vivante."

80   "[U]ne liqueur simplement nutritive" [...] "une liqueur active."

81   "Les accidents qu'éprouvent les femmes s'expliquent tout comme ceux des hommes. L'humeur qu'elles perdent étant moins précieuse, moins travaillée que le sperme de l'homme, sa perte ne les affaiblit peut-être pas aussi promptement; mais quand elles vont jusqu'à l'excès, le système nerveux étant plus faible chez elles, et naturellement disposé au spasme, les accidents sont violents."

82   "Le lait qu'elle refuse à son enfant se transforme en poison funeste, qui devient pour elle une source intarissable de douleurs et de tourments [...] Les marâtres qui s'affranchissent de ce devoir paient cher, pour l'ordinaire, ce délit de lèse-nature. Le lait dont elles ont la cruauté de priver leur fruit se porte indistinctement sur tous les organes et y exerce les plus terribles ravages. On a vu des femmes perdre la raison, l'ouïe, à la suite de quelques dépôts laiteux dans quelques parties du cerveau..."

83   "[U]n rêve de l'imagination et de l'ignorance."

84   "La résorption du lait est presque toujours nuisible à l'organe qui le sécrète, et retentit, en outre, sur la santé générale; les suites les plus communes de ce brusque tarissement se manifestent par les maladies connues sous le nom vulgaire de lait répandu, ou par des engorgements, des indurations, des abcès dans le parenchyme des seins; plus tard, par des squirres, des ulcères et quelquefois par une horrible maladie, le cancer! Le cancer n'a point de remèdes."

85   "[I]ls sont pâles, engourdis, paresseux, craintifs, lâches, dégradés au moral comme au physique." "Bientôt il tombe dans une complète débilité et la vie l'abandonne à son tour."

86   "Au moindre movement, le lait s'en échappait [du sein] comme d'un arrosoir [...] La pression en fait darder le lait en jets multiples, et dès que la pression vient à cesser, le lait coule constamment goutte à goutte, aussi la malade le recueille au moyen d'un vase qu'elle suspend à sa ceinture. Quand la malade se lève ou quand elle s'assied sur son lit, les gouttes de lait font place à des jets nombreux."

87   "Et tandis qu'on essayait ainsi de maîtriser, d'enrayer ce lait qui ne voulait pas se laisser faire, Geneviève avait des lamentations chantantes, et

renversée le corps en travers, s'enfonçait de plus en plus en un délire qui donnait l'épouvante."

88 "Et toujours, intarissable, en flux blancs et jaunes, le lait fuyait, et le long des flancs aussi il descendait, glissait, et par endroits sur le ventre il stagnait comme en une vasque profonde. Et Geneviève avait caché ses mains dans un effroi de les mouiller à cela, dans le dégoût de cette abondance superbe qui d'elle faisait irruption. Oh! ce lait qui refusait de finir, il lui paraissait que c'était du sang, qu'elle en perdait par entailles, qu'elle épuisait sa vie! Et dans sa tête cela dansait, se fondait, et il lui semblait soudain qu'en son cerveau aussi tout se liquéfiait."

89 "Mais quelle sève, quelle richesse! non jamais il ne s'était trouvé en face de pareille manifestation; du lait, du lait! à en nourrir une crèche! L'admirable prodigue! Ah, s'il avait su!"

90 "Oui, elle souffre, oui, tout est remis en cause, et c'est parce que nous ne sommes point avec le vrai, oh! cela seul le montre. On veut échapper au devoir pour lequel on est créé, remonter la nature, et voilà! C'est juste. Oh non, il ne fallait point! Le lait, son lait qui appartenait à notre fils, ce lait qu'il s'agit de bannir maintenant comme un poison, au lieu de le redouter et de le maudire, quelle joie, quelle sécurité il aurait values à la maison!"

91 "À la femme qui nourrit. Mère qui ne veux pas d'intermédiaire entre ton fils et toi, ce livre est ton triomphe et je te le dédie!"

92 "Sainte, purifiée, inaccessible, la femme qui nourrit. Son devoir n'admet pas de partage, l'amour qui l'a créé, la stérilise et la flétrit; elle est comme retirée dans la mission, l'esclavage, d'une virginité nouvelle…"

93 "[É]lève […] la sexualité humaine au niveau d'un rite magique, exorcisant la peur du ventre féminin qui devient le créateur des mondes, et aussi la terreur du sexe féminin, qui devient le tabernacle de la religion de fécondité."

94 "[L]e lien créé par l'allaitement au sein constitue un espace de jouissance possible risquant d'échapper à la symbolisation, risquant d'échapper au pouvoir social."

Chapter 4: Breast-Feeding, Literature, and Politics in the Third Republic

1 For more on the history of the wet-nursing industry, see Chapter 1 and also Fay-Sallois, 1980.

2 "[L]e départ de la mère pour Paris est souvent l'arrêt de mort de l'enfant."

3 "Voici donc 449 victimes de l'industrie de nourrices sur lieu, 449

infanticides avec préméditation [...] 449 meurtres sur lesquels on ferme les yeux et contre lesquels l'autorité locale reste désarmée."

4   "La patrie est en danger!"

5   "Le lait de la mère appartient à l'enfant."

6   "L'enfant, être humain membre de la société, doit être préservé dans son intégrité physique et morale et [...] les pouvoirs publics ont le droit et l'obligation d'intervenir pour assurer sa protection."

7   "[A]llaité par une nourrice n'ayant pas d'autre nourrisson." Loi Roussel quoted in Pinard, 1908.

8   "Les femmes qui ne veulent pas allaiter seront bien forcées à le faire le jour où la loi Roussel ne sera pas comme aujourd'hui impunément violée. Quand on ne permettra plus aux nourrices de venir se placer qu'après les sept mois révolus de leur enfant, alors les bureaux ne seront plus encombrés; et la nourrice mercenaire, cet être immoral qui, le plus souvent, tue son enfant en le privant de son lait pour en faire trafic, aura disparu. J'espère que, avec nos efforts à tous, les mères comprendront leur devoir, et que les droits sacrés de l'enfant seront enfin respectés." Dr Léon Petit, discours, "Le droit de l'enfant à sa mère."

9   "[Q]ue le lait de la femme appartient non à elle, mais à son enfant: qu'elle n'a pas le droit d'en trafiquer à sa guise, et que si elle peut être admise à le céder à un enfant étranger, c'est seulement lorsqu'il est légitime de présumer qu'il n'est plus *indispensable à la vie et à la santé du sien*." (Original emphasis.)

10   "Et ce fait prouve une fois de plus que, s'il est bon de changer, de modifier les lois, il est surtout indispensable de changer, de modifier les mœurs. Cette loi n'est pas exécutée, parce que les pauvres petits abandonnés ne peuvent réclamer, ils ne peuvent fonder un syndicat, ils se contentent de faire entendre quelques plaintes! ... avant de mourir."

11   "Ce qu'il fallait, c'étaient des mesures générales, des lois sauvant la nation: la femme aidée, protégée dès les premiers jours pénibles de la grossesse, soustraite aux dures besognes, devenue sacrée; la femme, plus tard, accouchée dans le calme, en secret si elle le désire, sans qu'on lui demande rien autre que d'être une mère; la femme et l'enfant, ensuite, soignés, secourus, pendant la convalescence, puis pendant les longs mois de l'allaitement, jusqu'au jour où, l'enfant mis au monde enfin, la femme puisse, de nouveau, être une épouse saine et vigoureuse. Il n'y avait là qu'une série de précautions à prendre, des maisons à créer, des refuges de grossesse, des maternités secrètes, des asiles de convalescence, sans parler des lois de protection ni des secours d'allaitement. Pour combattre le mal, affreux déchet des naissances, la mort soufflant par rafales sur les tout-petits, il n'existait qu'un moyen énergique, le prévenir."

12   "J'ai entendu mon père raconter que les meneuses, de son temps,

ramenaient chacun quatre ou cinq poupons à la fois. De vrais paquets qu'elles ficelaient et qu'elles portaient sous les bras. Dans les gares, elles les rangeaient sur les banquettes des salles d'attente; même, un jour, une meneuse de Rougemont en oublia un, et ça fit toute une histoire, parce qu'on retrouva l'enfant mort. Puis, il fallait voir, dans les trains, quel entassement de pauvres êtres, qui criaient la faim. […] Souvent, il en mourait, et l'on débarquait le petit cadavre à la prochaine station, on l'enterrait au cimetière le plus voisin. Vous comprenez dans quel état devaient arriver ceux qui ne mouraient pas en route. Chez nous, on soigne les cochons beaucoup mieux, car on ne les ferait sûrement pas voyager ainsi. Mon père disait que ça tirait les larmes des pierres… Mais, maintenant, il y a davantage de surveillance, les meneuses ne peuvent plus emmener qu'un poupon à la fois."

13 "De cette documentation de l'époque, reprise par Zola dans un souci de l'exactitude et sans la moindre exagération, il apparaît à l'évidence que ce massacre délibéré n'émouvait personne. Ni les bourgeoises qui doublaient les chances de mort de leurs propres enfants en les confiant à des nourrices 'sur lieu,' ni les nourrices qui savaient qu'elles avaient au moins une chance sur deux de ne pas revoir leurs propres enfants, ni les campagnardes qui bourraient les enfants de soupe dans des biberons et des petits pots crasseux, ni les meneuses, ni les sages-femmes qui étaient parfaitement informées de l'avenir des enfants déposés dans tous les Rougemont qui parsemaient la France."

14 "Toute mère a le devoir d'allaiter son enfant. L'enfant a droit au lait de sa mère."

15 "La liberté consiste à pouvoir faire tout ce qui ne nuit pas à autrui: ainsi l'exercice des droits naturels de chaque homme n'a de bornes que celles qui assurent aux autres Membres de la Société, la jouissance de ces mêmes droits."

16 "C'est l'affaire à l'Etat de protéger les nourrissons et de préserver les enfants, mais la loi et l'administration ne peuvent rien en ce qui concerne l'allaitement maternel."

17 "Si le droit d'allaiter pourrait faire sans dommage l'objet d'une protection législative, le droit à l'être ne le pourrait certainement pas, qui conduirait à imposer nécessairement aux mères d'allaiter. Une telle disposition constituerait d'ailleurs sans doute une atteinte aux libertés individuelles et à des normes supérieures et notamment aux articles 16 du Code civil renvoyant au droit au respect de l'intégrité corporelle."

18 "Et c'est pourquoi, les législateurs me paraissant sans force, je voudrais qu'on confiât la tâche aux moralistes, aux écrivains, aux poètes."

19 "[T]out changerait, si l'on persuadait à nos jeunes et jolies dames que rien n'est beau […] comme les nombreuses familles."

20 "Chose horrible! il fallut, / Pour sauver le vieux toit, la vache et le

bahut, / Que la mère quittât son pays, sa chaumière, / Son enfant, les yeux clos encore à la lumière, / Et qui, dans son berceau, gémissait, l'innocent! / Qu'elle vendît, hélas! son lait, plus que son sang, / Et que, le front courbé par cet acte servile, / Douloureuse, elle prît le chemin de la ville."

21 "La nourrice voulut revenir au plus vite / Au fils qu'elle pouvait allaiter aujourd'hui, / À l'enfant campagnard, qui se portait bien, lui! / [...] C'est le terme à présent de sa longue souffrance. / Elle va voir son fils! – Enfin, ô délivrance!"

22 "Et dans l'ombre, parmi les choses de rebut, / Sale, brisé, couvert de toiles d'araignée, / – Objet horrible aux yeux d'une mère indignée, / Et qu'on avait jeté dans le coin sans remords – / L'humble berceau en osier du petit enfant mort. / Elle tomba. C'était la fin du sacrifice."

23 "Et depuis lors, on voit, à Caen, dans un hospice, / Tenant fixe sur vous ses yeux secs et brulants, / Une femme encor jeune avec des cheveux blancs, / Qui cherche de la main sa mamelle livide / Et balance toujours du pied un berceau vide."

24 "Et rien ne contractait les traits de Marianne; elle n'eût pas même un étonnement et l'homme qui lui apportait cette nouvelle en resta stupide. Vraiment, son petit enfant venait d'être en quelques jours étouffé par le croup? Son petit! Quel petit? Maintenant il y avait cinq ans que Marianne était chez le baron Devin: et jamais elle n'avait senti l'ennui du pays, un besoin de revoir ou de s'enquérir de son enfant: non, sa vie ne l'intéressait point; non, il n'existait pas pour elle, l'enfant de là-bas! [...] Son enfant, le petit du village? Celui auprès duquel elle eût été condamnée à vivre malheureuse et misérable elle aussi? ah! oublié, renié, celui-là!"

25 "[Q]uant à la nourrice sur lieu, c'est une transaction honteuse, une source incalculable de maux, souvent même un double crime, le double sacrifice consenti de l'enfant de la mère et de l'enfant de la nourrice."

26 "C'était un garçon, de trois mois au plus, l'air solide et fort. Un instant, il leva la tête pour demander:
"C'est bien à vous, au moins, cet enfant-là?
– Oh! monsieur! ... Où voulez-vous donc que je l'aie pris.
– Dame! ma fille, ça se prête." (Zola, n.d., 399)

27 "Puis, un frisson l'avait saisi lorsque la meneuse s'était tournée vers le bel enfant bien sage dont elle parlait de débarrasser la nourrice. Et il la revoyait avec les cinq autres, à la gare Saint-Lazare, s'envolant, emportant chacune un nouveau-né, telles que des corneilles de massacre et de deuil. C'était la rafle qui recommençait [...] avec la menace cette fois d'un meurtre double comme disait le docteur, deux enfants en danger de mort, celui de la nourrice et celui de la mère."

28 "Un si bel enfant! c'est un vent qui souffle, que veux-tu! Et puis, enfant de nourrice, enfant de sacrifice."

29   "Le brusque souvenir lui était revenu de sa conversation avec Boutan […] le crime commun des deux mères, risquant chacune la mort de son enfant, la mère oisive qui achetait le lait d'une autre, la mère vénale qui vendait le sien. Il eut froid au cœur … Et quel serait le destin, quel vent soufflerait d'une société à ce point mal faite et corrompue, sacrifiant l'un ou l'autre, les deux peut-être? Les gens, les choses s'assombrirent, lui firent horreur."

30   "[O]ù il est exclusivement parlé de nourrices qui tuent."

31   "[Ô] François Coppée! […] Tu sais ce que c'est qu'une mère! Tu sais ce que c'est que la patrie […] et tu sais surtout, ce que c'est d'écrire!"

32   "[L]es personnages ne sont plus que l'incarnation d'une idée."

33   "Et c'est pourquoi, les législateurs me paraissant sans force, je voudrais qu'on confiât la tâche aux moralistes, aux écrivains, aux poètes."

34   "[E]lles font un mauvais calcul, car l'allaitement fatigue la mère mais ne l'abîme pas, au contraire, il est utile à la race entière."

35   For more, see Chapter 1.

36   "Si ta mère ne peut te nourrir, si ton père te maltraite, si tu es nu, si tu as faim, viens, mon fils, les portes sont toutes grandes ouvertes, et la France est au seuil pour t'embrasser et te recevoir. Elle ne rougira jamais, cette grande mère, de prendre pour toi les soins de la nourrice, elle te fera de sa main héroïque la soupe du soldat, et si elle n'avait pas de quoi envelopper, réchauffer tes petits membres engourdis, elle arracherait plutôt un pan de son drapeau."

37   Translation paraphrased from the King James Bible.

38   "[U]ne puissante nourrice qui nous allaite par millions."

39   See www.wikiart.org/en/honore-daumier/the-republic-1848.

40   "Une Marianne-Mère ouvre sa puissante et généreuse poitrine à des enfants qui s'y alimentent. La symétrie, dans cette œuvre magnifique, introduit naturellement à l'idée d'Egalité. Que ces deux 'enfants de la République' évoquent les principales classes sociales est possible, mais non certain. En tout cas, l'idée de générosité et d'équité économiques, que nous avions suggérée, se trouve ici parfaitement exposée. Le sein est pouvoir de donner un bienfait social et politique partagé."

41   For more on breast-feeding in France during the Revolutionary period, see Chapter 1.

42   For more on the history of the Society of Maternal Charity, see Chapter 2.

43   "L'assistance est due à l'enfant. Il a droit à une protection entière, complète, permanente."

44   "Il me semble que nourrir ses enfants est pour notre pays le plus grand intérêt et le premier devoir. Ce n'est pas le pan du drapeau dont parle Michelet que réclame l'enfant, c'est … le lait de sa mère auquel il a droit."

45   "[P]our forcer les mères qui acceptent ce secours à alimenter elles-mêmes au sein."

46   "On aura peine à croire pourtant que Zola n'ait pas fait un choix significatif, puisque le mari de Marianne, Matthieu, a trois frères nommés Marc, Luc et Jean (les quatre Evangélistes) et que leur nom de famille est Froment (symbole d'une fécondité agricole aussi exaltée tout au long de l'œuvre que la fécondité des hommes)."

47   "Toute blanche également, le visage adouci, éclairé d'une aube dernière sous des bandeaux de soie fine, elle était telle qu'un de ces marbres sacrés dont le temps a raviné les traits, sans pouvoir en détruire la tranquille splendeur de vie, quelque Cybèle féconde, retrouvée dans son ferme dessin, revivant en plein jour."

48   "[C]ouronnée d'épis de blé, ce qui lui vaut le titre, bien connu encore aujourd'hui des philatelists, de timbre 'à la Cérès,' du nom de la déesse romaine des moissons."

49   "[N]e portera pas un bonnet rouge. Elle ne sera pas une vivandière, mais une mère féconde, sereine et glorieuse, qui aura des fêtes et des sourires pour ses enfants."

50   "Dans la nappe de clair soleil qui dorait le lit, elle rayonnait elle-même de santé, de force et d'espoir. Jamais ses lourds cheveux bruns n'avaient coulé de sa nuque si puissamment, jamais ses grands yeux n'avaient souri d'une gaieté plus vaillante. Et, avec son visage de bonté et d'amour, d'une correction si saine, si solide, elle était la fécondité elle-même, la bonne déesse aux chairs éclatantes, au corps parfait, d'une noblesse souveraine. Une vénération l'envahit, il l'adora, comme un dévot mis en présence de son Dieu, au seuil du mystère."

51   "Et c'était là le flot de lait coulant par le monde, le flot d'éternelle vie pour l'éternelle moisson des êtres."

52   "[P]réfère une poitrine opulente, plus maternelle, promesse de générosité et d'abondance."

53   "Il n'est pas, aux colonies, de race plus féconde que la race française, elle qui paraît être devenue stérile sur son antique sol. Et nous pullulerons, et nous emplirons le monde."

54   "La nappe du lait ruisselant emporte dans son irrésistible expansion la race pullulante des Froment lancé à la conquête de la terre."

55   "Par-dessus les mers, le lait avait coulé, du vieux sol de France, jusqu'aux immensités de l'Afrique vierge, la jeune et géante France de demain."

56   "Sous forme d'image féminine enfin, Marianne, embellie et enlaidie suivant l'opinion que l'on défend, représente commodément le régime dans la caricature politique, qui fleurit désormais librement."

Conclusion

1   "[U]ne pièce à thèse; c'est surtout une thèse et on regrette que la pièce
en soit négligée."

2   "Je suis le premier homme de lettres à avoir écrit des œuvres littéraires
sur le danger des nourrices, sur le danger des hommes blessés par l'amour;
M. Brieux a *vulgarisé* mes sujets."

3   For accounts of Hepp's duels, see *Le Cri du peuple*, May 1, 1884, and *Le
Figaro*, September 11, 1886.

4   "[L]orsque la mère est dans l'impossibilité absolue de remplir son devoir,
il y a le biberon, qui, bien tenu, employé soigneusement, avec du lait stérilisé,
donnent des résultats suffisants."

5   "Il n'a pas compris les femmes, ce sublime Rousseau [...] Il a fait des
nourrices croyant faire des mères. Il a pris le sein maternel pour l'âme
génératrice. Le plus spiritualiste des philosophes du siècle dernier a été
matérialiste sur la question des femmes."

Works Cited

Adams, Christine. *Poverty, Charity and Motherhood: Maternal Societies in Nineteenth-Century France.* Urbana: University of Illinois Press, 2010.

Agulhon, Maurice. "Esquisse pour une archéologie de la République: l'allégorie civique féminine." *Annales. Économies, Sociétés, Civilisations.* 28.1, 1973, 5–34.

———. *Marianne au pouvoir: l'imagerie et la symbolique républicaines de 1880 à 1914.* Paris: Flammarion, 1989.

Agulhon, Maurice, and Pierre Bonté, *Marianne: les visages de la République.* Paris: Gallimard, 1992.

L'allégorie dans la peinture: la représentation de la charité au XVIIᵉ siècle. Musée des Beaux-Arts de Caen, July 27–October 13, 1986.

Alliance nationale pour l'accroissement de la population française. *Bulletin de l'Alliance nationale pour l'accroissement de la population française* 1.4 (October 15, 1899), 46–47.

Andréoli, M. "Un roman épistolaire: les mémoires de deux jeunes mariées." *L'Année balzacienne*, 1987, 255–95.

Assemblée nationale. "Le temps de l'invention (1789–1799)." www2. assemblee-nationale.fr/decouvrir-l-assemblee/histoire/histoire-de-l-assemblee-nationale/le-temps-de-l-invention-1789-1799. Accessed December 20, 2021.

Aubry, Étienne. "Adieux to the Wet Nurse." Painting. Oil. 1776. Clark Institute of Art, Massachusetts, USA.

Baguley, David. *Fécondité d'Émile Zola: roman à thèse, évangile, mythe.* Toronto: University of Toronto Press, 1973.

Balzac, Honoré de. *La Comédie humaine.* Ed. Pierre-Georges Castex. 2 vols. Paris: Gallimard, 1976.

———. *Correspondance.* Ed. R. Pierrot and Hervé Yon. Paris: Gallimard, 2017.

———. *The Lily of the Valley and Other Stories.* Trans. James Waring. Philadelphia: Gebbie Publishing Co., 1898.

———. *Mémoires de deux jeunes mariées.* Ed. Samuel S. de Sacy. Preface by Bernard Pingaud. Paris: Gallimard, 1981.

———. *Memoirs of Two Young Married Women.* Trans. Katharine Prescott Wormeley. Boston: Roberts Brothers, 1894.

———. *The Two Young Brides*. Trans. Mary Loyd. Introduction by Henry James. New York: Appleton, 1902.

Baudoin, Sébastien, "La Figure de la mère dans les écrits personnels de Lamartine: la muse et l'initiatrice." In *Les relations familiales dans les écritures de l'intime du XIXe siècle français*. Eds. Simone Bernard-Griffiths and Daniel Madelénat. Clermont-Ferrand: Maison des Science de l'Homme, 2016, 217–35.

Bayle, Antoine Laurent Jessé, and C.-M. Gilbert, *Dictionnaire de médecine usuelle et domestique* ... vol. 2, G–Z. Paris: Veuve Lacour, 1858–59.

Bayle-Mouillard, É. *Manuel des nourrices*. Paris: J. Renouard, 1834.

Bécquet de Vienne, Marie. "Assistance aux mères." *Revue philanthropique* 2 (November 1897).

Beizer, Janet. *Ventriloquized Bodies: Narratives of Hysteria in Nineteenth-Century France*. Ithaca, NY: Cornell University Press, 1993.

Berthier, Philippe. "Accoucher au masculin (Balzac, *Mémoires de Deux Jeunes Mariées*)." In Jean-Marie Roulin, *Corps, littérature et société*. Saint-Étienne: Publications de l'Université de Saint-Étienne, 2005, 293–306.

Bertillon, J. *Le problème de la dépopulation*. Paris: Colin, 1897.

Bertrand-Jennings, Chantal. *L'Eros et la femme chez Zola*. Paris: Klincksieck, 1977.

Besnard, l'abbé. *Périls auxquels sont exposés les enfans que leurs mères refusent d'allaiter; malheurs que, par ce refus ces mères attirent sur elles-mêmes*. Paris: Libraire de Mme Huzard, 1825.

Béthléem, Louis. *Romans à lire et romans à proscrire. Essai de classification au point de vue moral des principaux romans et romanciers (1500–1928)*. Paris: Éditions de la Revue des lectures, 1928.

Blavet, Emile (pseud. Parisis). "La Vie parisienne: l'Épuisé." *Le Figaro* (July 10, 1888).

Bloy, Léon. *Journal inédit*. Paris, 1899.

Blum, Carol. *Rousseau and the Republic of Virtue: The Language of Politics in the French Revolution*. Ithaca, NY: Cornell University Press, 1986.

Boissin, F. "Compte rendu de l'Épuisé." *Polybiblion: revue bibliographique universelle* 53, 1888.

Bonnetain, Paul. *Charlot s'amuse*. 2nd ed. Brussels: H. Kistemaeckers, 1883.

Boon, Sonia. "Maternalising the (Female) Breast: A Comparison of Marie-Angélique Anel Le Rebours, *Avis aux mères qui veulent nourrir leurs enfans* (1767) and La Leche League International's *The Womanly Art of Breastfeeding* (1963)." *Limina: A Journal of Historical and Cultural Studies* 15, 2009, 1–18.

Boutin, Aimée. *City of Noise: Sound and Nineteenth-Century Paris*. Urbana: University of Illinois Press, 2015.

Briquet, Pierre, *Traité clinique et thérapeutique de l'hystérie*. Paris: J.-B. Baillière, 1859.

Brouard-Arends, Isabelle. *Vies et images maternelles dans la littérature française du dix-huitième siècle*. Oxford: Voltaire Foundation, 1991.

Bru, Monsieur, ancien chirurgien d'armée & d'infanterie, Maître en l'art & science de la Chirurgie de la ville de Montauban, & accoucheur. *Avis aux mères qui se proposent de nourrir leurs enfans, sur un moyen propre à les favoriser dans cette pénible fonction*. Toulouse: Chez l'auteur, 1780.

Bulletin de l'Alliance nationale pour l'accroissement de la population française 4 (October 15, 1899). https://gallica.bnf.fr/ark:/12148/bpt6k5777067z/f1.image. Accessed December 20, 2021.

Burton, June K. *Napoleon and the Woman Question: Discourses of the Other Sex in French Education, Medicine, and Medical Law, 1799–1815.* Lubbock: Texas Tech University Press, 2007.

Cabanis, P. J. G. *Rapports du physique et du moral de l'homme et lettre sur les causes premières.* Paris: J.-B. Baillière, 1844.

Calley Galitz, Kathryn. "Nourishing the Body Politic: Images of Breast-Feeding in the French Salons, 1789–1814." In Patricia R. Ivinski, Harry C. Payne, Kathryn Calley Galitz, and Richard Rand. *Farewell to the Wet Nurse: Étienne Aubry and Images of Breast-Feeding in Eighteenth-Century France.* Williamstown, MA: Clark Institute, 1998, 25–35.

Campan, Madame, *Journal anecdotique de Mme Campan, ou Souvenirs, recueillis dans ses entretiens, par M. Maigne.* Paris: Baudouin frères, 1824.

Carraud, Zulma, and Honoré de Balzac. *Correspondance inédite avec Madame Zulma Carraud.* Paris: Colin, 1935.

Charpentier, J.-L. "Les Médecins et l'idée scientifique à la scène." *Revue du mois* 6, 1908, 457–80.

Chateaubriand, François-René de, *Génie du christianisme.* Édition complète. Paris: INALF, 1961 [Reprint of Paris: Imprimerie Migneret, 4 vols. 1803].

———. *Mémoires d'outre-tombe.* Ed. M. Levaillant. 12 vols. Paris: Flammarion, 1948.

"Chez Monsieur Hepp." *Le Matin* (May 10, 1890).

Chung, Ye Young. "Mémoires de deux jeunes mariées: paroles au féminin." *L'Année balzacienne* 1.6, 2005, 323–46.

Coffignon, Ali. *L'enfant à Paris: Paris-vivant.* Paris: E. Kolb, 1889.

"La Colère de M. Hepp." *La Croix* (October 28, 1887), 2.

Coles, Prophecy. *The Shadow of the Second Mother: Nurses and Nannies in Theories of Infant Development.* New York: Routledge, 2015.

"Compte rendu du *Lait d'une autre.*" *L'année littéraire* 7, 1891, 199.

Conner, Tom. *The Dreyfus Affair and the Rise of the French Public Intellectual.* Jefferson, NC: McFarland & Co., Inc., 2014.

Conseil général du département de la Seine, 3e session de 1882.

"Constitution de 1791." *Le Conseil Constitutionnel.* www.conseil-constitutionnel. fr/les-constitutions-dans-l-histoire/constitution-de-1791. Accessed July 20, 2018.

Coppée, François. *Les Humbles.* Paris: A. Lemerre, 1872.

Counter, Andrew J. "Zola's *fin-de-siècle* Reproductive Politics." *French Studies* 68.2, 2014, 193–208.

Cova, Anna. *Maternité et droits des femmes en France (XIXᵉ–XXᵉ siècles).* Paris: Economica, 1997.

Daubenton, Mme. *Zélie dans le désert.* Paris: 1787.

Davis, Peggy. "La quête de primitivisme ou le doute envers la civilisation: l'illustration visuelle dans Les Incas de Marmontel (1777) et Atala de Chateaubriand (1801)." *Études littéraires* 37.3, 2006, 117–44.

Debay, Auguste. *Hygiène et physiologie du mariage: histoire naturelle et médicale de l'homme et de la femme mariés, dans ses plus curieux détails; Hygiène spéciale de la femme enceinte et du nouveau-né (29e édition)*. Paris: E. Dentu, 1862.

de Ceuleneer, Adolf. "La Charité romaine dans la littérature et dans l'art." *Annales de l'Académie royale d'archéologie de Belgique* 67, 1919, 175–205.

Décret relatif à l'organisation de la charité maternelle, 25 juillet 1811. In *Législation charitable: ou, Recueil de lois, arrêtés, décrets, ordonnances royales, avis du Conseil d'État, circulaires, décisions et instructions des ministres de l'intérieur et des finances, arrêts de la Cour des comptes, etc., etc., qui régissent les établissements de bienfaisance, mise en ordre et annotée* … Paris: Alexandre Heois, 1843.

Décret relatif à l'organisation des secours à accorder annuellement aux enfants, aux vieillards et aux indigents. Convention nationale du 28 juin au 8 juillet 1793. www.onpe.gouv.fr/historique#. Accessed December 20, 2021.

Deleurye, François Ange, fils, Conseiller-Chirurgien ordinaire du Roi en son Châtelet de Paris. *La Mère selon l'ordre de la nature, avec un traité sur les maladies des enfants.* Paris: Chez Hérissant, père, 1772.

Denton, Margaret Fields. "A Woman's Place: The Gendering of Genres in Post-Revolutionary French Painting." *Art History* 21.2, 1998, 219–46.

Descaves, Lucien. *La vie douloureuse de Marceline Desbordes-Valmore.* Paris: Éditions d'art et de littérature, 1910.

Desplace, J.-B. *Des Dangers de l'envoi en nourrice, conférence publique et gratuite à l'Hôtel-de-ville de Mâcon.* Mâcon: Bonnin-Julien.1875.

"Les Deuils." *Les Annales politiques et littéraires* (October 12, 1924).

Diderot, Denis. *Œuvres. Salons: Salon de 1765. Essai sur la peinture, pour faire suite au salon de 1765.* Paris: Chez J. L. J. Brière. www.google.co.uk/books/edition/Salons_Salon_de_1761_1765_Essai_sur_la_p/qJVAAAAAYAAJ?hl=en&gbpv=1&printsec=frontcover. Accessed December 20, 2021.

———. *Supplément à l'Encyclopédie ou Dictionnaire raisonné des sciences, des arts et des métiers* (vol. 1). Amsterdam: Chez M. M. Rey, 1776. www.biodiversitylibrary.org/item/205238#page/9/mode/1up. Accessed December 20, 2021.

Didierjean-Jouveau, Claude-Suzanne. "L'histoire de l'allaitement au XXᵉ siècle." 2003. www.claude-didierjean-jouveau.fr/2016/06/12/histoire-de-lallaitement-20-siecle/. Accessed December 20, 2021.

Donné, Alfred. *Conseils aux mères sur la manière d'élever les enfans nouveau-nés, ou de l'Éducation physique des enfans du premier âge,* par Al[fred] Donné, docteur en médecine, ex-chef de la clinique de la Faculté de Paris, professeur particulier de microscopie, etc. Paris: J.-B. Baillière, 1842.

Dulaurent, Citoyen. *La bonne mère, discours prononcé dans la section des Tuileries, à la fête de la raison, le 20 frimaire, l'an 2e de la république une & indivisible.* Paris: de l'Imprimerie nationale exécutive du Louvre, 1793. https://gallica.bnf.fr/ark:/12148/bpt6k42842d.texteImage. Accessed December 20, 2021.

Dumesnil, R. *L'Époque réaliste et naturaliste.* Paris: Jules Tallandier, 1945.

Duncan, Carol. "Happy Mothers and Other New Ideas in Eighteenth-Century French Art." In *The Aesthetics of Power: Essays in Critical Art History.* Cambridge: Cambridge University Press, 1993, 3–26.

du Tillet, Jacques. "Théâtres." *Revue politique et littéraire: revue bleue.* Paris: Bureau des revues, 1901, 250–52.

Encyclopédie, ou dictionnaire raisonné des sciences, des arts et des métiers, par une Société de Gens de lettres, published under the direction of Denis Diderot and Jean le Rond d'Alembert. 17 vols. text; 11 vols. plates. Paris: Chez Briasson, 1751–72.

Epinay, Louise-Florence Tardieu d'. *Les Pseudo-mémoires de Mme d'Epinay. Histoire de Madame de Montbrillant.* 3 vols. Paris: Gallimard, 1951.

Escholier, Raymond. *Daumier et son monde.* Paris: Éditions Berger-Levrault, 1965.

Fay-Sallois, Fanny. *Les Nourrices à Paris au XIXe siècle.* Paris: Payot, 1980.

Flandrin, Jean-Louis. *Familles: parenté, maison, sexualité dans l'ancienne société.* Paris: Hachette, 1976.

Flaubert, Gustave. *Mémoires d'un fou.* Paris: Arvensa Editions, 2014.

Flouest, Joseph. "Un enfant que l'on ramène de nourrice, et qui se refuse aux embrassements de sa mère." Later renamed "Retour de nourrice." Painting. Oil. 1804. Musée-Château de Dieppe.

Fort, Bernadette. "Greuze and the Ideology of Infant Nursing in Eighteenth-Century France." In Anya Muller, *Fashioning Childhood in the Eighteenth Century: Age and Identity.* Burlington, VT: Ashgate, 2006, 117–34.

Foucault, Michel. *Les Anormaux. Cours au Collège de France, 1974–1975.* Édition numérique réalisée en août 2012 à partir de l'édition CD-ROM. Le Foucault Électronique. Paris: Gallimard, 2001.

Francis, John Edward. *The Athenaeum* (January–June 1908).

Franklin, Alfred. *La Vie privée d'autrefois: arts et métiers, modes, mœurs, usages des Parisiens, du XIIe au XVIIIe siècle,* d'après des documents originaux ou inédits par Alfred Franklin … 27 vols. Paris: E. Plon, Nourrit, & Cie, 1887–1902.

Freud, Sigmund. *The Freud Reader.* Ed. and trans. Peter Gay. New York: W. W. Norton, 1989.

———. *Three Essays on the Theory of Sexuality.* London: Imago Publishing Company, 1949.

Fuchs, Rachel G. *Poor and Pregnant in Paris: Strategies for Survival in the Nineteenth Century.* New Brunswick, NJ: Rutgers University Press, 1992.

Gachet, Marie-Hélène. "Évolution d'un sujet iconographique de l'antiquité à nos jours: la Caritas romana." *Travaux de l'Institut d'histoire de l'art de Lyon* 7, 1984, 82–86.

Gaultier de Claubry, Charles Daniel. *Nouvel avis aux mères qui veulent nourrir.* Paris: Lottin le jeune, 1783.

Genlis, Stéphanie de. *Adèle et Théodore, ou lettres sur l'éducation.* Paris: Crapelet, 1801.

Gérard, Marguerite. "Un enfant amené par sa nourrice à sa mère, qu'il ne veut pas reconnaître." Painting. Oil. Salon of 1804. Location unknown.

———. "Une mère nourrice présentant son sein à son enfant, que lui amène une gouvernante." Painting. Oil. Salon of 1804. Musée Fragonard in Grasse, France, with the title "Les Premiers Pas, ou la Mère nourrice."

Goncourt, Edmond, and Jules Goncourt. *La Femme au XVIIIe siècle.* Paris: Flammarion, 1982 [1862].

Gros, Dominique. *Le Sein dévoilé*. Paris: Éditions de la Seine, 1987.

Guéhenno, Jean. *Jean-Jacques*. vol. 3. *1758–1778: Grandeur et misère d'un esprit*. Paris: Gallimard, 1952.

Guillemin, Henri, *Le Jocelyn de Lamartine, étude historique et critique*. Paris: Boivin & Cⁱᵉ, 1936.

Gutwirth, Madelyn, *Twilight of the Goddess: Women and Representation in the French Revolutionary Era*. New Brunswick, NJ: Rutgers University Press, 1992.

Hauser, Fernand. "L'Incident Hepp-Brieux." *Echo de Paris* (November 6, 1901).

Hemmings, F. W. J., *Émile Zola*. Oxford: Clarendon Press, 1953.

Hepp, A. *Le lait d'une autre: roman sur les dangers de l'allaitement mercenaire*. Paris: E. Dentu, 1891.

———. *Les Quotidiennes*. Paris: Flammarion, 1898–99.

Hérault de Séchelles, Marie-Jean. *Discours prononcés par Hérault-Séchelles, président de la convention nationale, le 10 Auguste 1793, a la fête de l'unité et de l'indivisibilité de la République française, L'An IIᵉ de la République française, une et indivisible*. s.n. 1793.

Herbinet, Étienne (ed.) *D'amour et de lait: ouvrage collectif sur l'allaitement*. Paris: Stock, 1980.

Herold, A. Ferdinand. "Les Théâtres." *Mercure de France* 49, 1908, 235–43.

Herz, Micheline. "The Angelism of Madame de Ségur." Yale French Studies 27, *Women Writers*, 1961, 12–21.

Herzog-Evans, Martine. *Allaitement maternel et droit*. Paris: Harmattan, 2007.

Hugo, Victor, *Les Contemplations*, Ed. J. Vianey, Paris: Hachette, 1922.

———. *Feuilles d'automne*. Paris: Charpentier, 1846.

———. *Œuvres complètes*. 48 vols. Paris: Édition Hetzel–Quantin/L. Hébert Libraire, 1962.

———. *Les Rayons et les ombres*. In *Œuvres poétiques*. Paris: Gallimard, 1964, vol. 1. *Informations*.

Irigaray, Luce, "Ce sexe qui n'en est pas un." In *New French Feminisms: An Anthology*. Ed. and trans. Elaine Marks and Isabelle de Courtivron. New York: Schocken Books, 1980.

Ivinski, Patricia. "Maternal versus Mercenary Nursing: Popular Debate and Artistic Representation." In Patricia R. Ivinski, Harry C. Payne, Kathryn Calley Galitz, and Richard Rand. *Farewell to the Wet Nurse: Étienne Aubry and Images of Breast-Feeding in Eighteenth-Century France*. Williamstown, MA: Clark Institute, 1998, 9–17.

Jacobus, Mary. "Incorruptible Milk: Breast-Feeding and the French Revolution." In *First Things: The Maternal Imaginary in Literature, Art and Psychoanalysis*. New York: Routledge, 1995.

Joubert, Laurent, *Erreurs populaires du fait de la médecine et régime de santé*. Bordeaux: S. Millanges, 1578.

Journal des arts, des sciences et de littérature 394 (January 10, 1805), 80–81.

Kayser, Christine (ed.) *L'Enfant chéri au siècle des Lumières; après l'Emile*. Museum exhibition catalogue, Musée-promenade de Marly-le-Roi–Louveciennes, 2003.

Klein, Melanie. *Envy and Gratitude*. London, The Hogarth Press, 1946.

Knibiehler, Yvonne, and Catherine Fouquet. *Histoire des mères du Moyen Age à nos jours*. Paris: Editions Montalba, 1980.

Kristeva, Julia. "About Chinese Women." In *The Kristeva Reader*. Ed. Toril Moi. New York: Columbia University Press, 1986.

Lacassagne, Jean-Pierre (ed.) *Histoire d'une amitié (d'après une correspondance inédite 1836–1866): Pierre Leroux et George Sand*. Paris: Klincksieck, 1973.

Lamartine, Alphonse de, *Les Confidences*. New ed. Paris: Hachette & c^{ie}/Furne, Jouvet & Cie, 1879.

———. *Œuvres complètes*. 7 vols. Paris: Chez l'auteur, 1860.

Landais, Pierre. *Dissertation sur les avantages de l'allaitement des enfans par leurs mères; ouvrage qui a été couronné par la Faculté de Médecine de Paris, dans sa Séance publique, le 9 décembre 1779*. Geneva and Paris: Chez Méquignon, 1781.

Landon, Charles Paul, *Annales du musée … salon de 1810*. Paris: Imprimerie Chaignieau (Aîné), 1810.

Las Cases, Emmanuel-Auguste-Dieudonné. *Le Mémorial de Sainte Hélène*. 4 vols. Paris: E. Bourdin, 1812.

Lastinger, Valerie. "Professionalising Motherhood: Cora Millet-Robinet and the Maternal as Profession." *French Cultural Studies* 23.3, 2012, 175–89.

———. "Re-Defining Motherhood: Breast-Feeding and the French Enlightenment." *Women's Studies* 25.6, 1996, 603–17.

La Leche League International, *The Womanly Art of Breastfeeding*. New York: Plume, 2004.

Lefébure, H. "L'Opinion d'Émile Zola sur l'allaitement maternel." *La Fronde* 714.1 (November 19, 1899).

Legouvé, Gabriel. *Le Mérite des femmes: poëme*. Paris: L'Edition de Paris: Chez Louis, An IX [1800–1801].

Le Rebours, Marie Angélique Anel, *Avis aux mères qui veulent nourrir leurs enfans*. 2nd ed. (*Revue et considérablement augmentée*). Paris: Didot le jeune, 1770.

———. *Avis aux mères qui veulent nourrir leurs enfans*. 3rd ed. (*Revue et considérablement augmentée*). Paris: Didot le jeune, 1775.

———. *Avis aux mères qui veulent nourrir leurs enfans*. 5th ed. (*Revue et considérablement augmentée*). Paris: Chez Théophile Barrois, An VII [1798].

LeNoir, Jean-Charles-Pierre. *Détails sur quelques établissemens de la ville de Paris, demandé par sa Majesté Impériale la Rein de Hongrie … Paris: 1780.

Leroy-Allais, Jeanne. *Les droits de l'enfant*. Paris: Montgredien & Cie, 1900.

Lesbazeilles, Eugène. "Gabriel Legouvé." *Le Magasin pittoresque*, publié … sous la direction de M. Édouard Charton. Paris: 1886, 343–44.

Lescure, Mathurin. *François Coppée: l'homme, la vie et l'œuvre (1842–1889)*. Paris: A. Lemerre, 1889.

Levy, Darline Gray, Harriet Branson Applewhite, and Mary Durham Johnson, *Women in Revolutionary Paris, 1789–1795*. Urbana: University of Illinois Press, 1980.

Likierman, Meira, *Melanie Klein: Her Work in Context*. London, Continuum, 2001.

Lorant, André. "Balzac et le plaisir." *L'Année balzacienne* 17, 1996, 287–304.

Lorimier, Henriette. "A Young Woman Watching A Goat Nurse Her Child." Painting. Oil. Salon of 1804, Paris. Location unknown.

Malinas, C. "Le Culte du sein dans *Fécondité*." *Cahiers Naturalistes* 60, 1986, 171–83.

Marchal, Bertrand (ed.) *Mallarmé, mémoire de la critique.* Paris: Presses universitaires de Paris–Sorbonne, 1998.

Marmontel, Jean-François. *Les Incas, ou la Destruction de l'Empire du Pérou.* Lima: Travaux de l'Institut français d'études andines, 1991 [Frankfurt & Leipzig: H.-L. Broenner, 1777].

Mayer, Constance. "The Happy Mother (La Mère heureuse)." Painting. Oil. Salon of 1810. Musée du Louvre, Paris.

———. "The Unfortunate Mother (La Mère infortunée)." Painting. Oil. Salon of 1810. Musée du Louvre, Paris.

Mayer-Robin, Carmen. "The 'African Pages' of Zola's *Fécondité*: Testimony to Colonial Politics and Attitudes about Race during the French Third Republic." *Romance Notes* 7.1, 2006, 5–14.

———. "The Formidable Flow of Milk in *Le Docteur Pascal* and *Fécondité*: Two Feminine Allegories for the 'République en marche.'" *Excavatio* 13, 2000, 69–80.

Menville, Charles François. *Histoire médicale et philosophique de la femme considérée dans toutes les époques principales de sa vie.* Paris: Amyot, 1845.

Mercier, Louis-Sébastien. *Paris pendant la révolution (1790–1798): ou, le nouveau Paris.* Paris: Poulet-Malassis, 1862 [1798].

———. *Tableau de Paris.* Amsterdam: s.n., 1782–83.

Mérot, Alain. "Préface." In *L'allégorie dans la peinture: la représentation de la charité au XVIIe siècle.* Musée des Beaux-Arts de Caen (July 27–October 13, 1986).

Michelet, Jules. *The People.* Trans. John P. McKay. Urbana: University of Illinois Press, 1973.

———. *Le Peuple.* Paris: Calmann Lévy, 1877.

Millet-Robinet, Cora. *Conseils aux jeunes femmes sur leur condition et leurs devoirs de mère, pendant l'allaitement.* Paris: Bouchard-Huzard, 1841.

Millet-Robinet, Cora, and Émile Allix (Médecin–inspecteur du service de la protection des enfants et des crèches à Paris), *Le Livre des jeunes mères: la nourrice et le nourrisson.* 5th ed. Paris: Librairie Agricole de la Maison Rustique, 1897.

Mirbeau, Octave. *Chroniques du diable.* Besançon: Presses universitaires de Franche-Comté, 1995.

Monot, Charles. *De l'industrie des nourrices et de la mortalité des petits enfants.* Paris: Achille Faure, 1867.

———. *De la mortalité excessive des enfants pendant la première année de leur existence, ses causes et des moyens de la restreindre.* Paris: J.-B. Baillière, 1872.

Montaigne, Michel de. *Les Essais: édition nouvelle, trouvée après le deceds de l'autheur, revueuë & augmentée par luy d'un tiers plus qu'aux précédentes impressions.* 2 vols. Paris: Chez Abel L'Angelier, 1595. https://gallica.bnf.fr/ark:/12148/bpt6k52511h. Accessed December 20, 2021.

Muhlfeld, Lucien. "Chronique de la littérature." *La Revue blanche. Nouvelle série* 1.78, 1891.

Nicolas, Pierre-François, *Le cri de la nature, en faveur des enfans nouveaux nés; ouvrage dans lequel on expose les regles diététiques que les femmes doivent suivre pendant leur grossesse, & pendant leurs couches; les avantages & les douceurs qu'elles trouveront à nourrir leurs enfans; & les dangers qu'elles courront, en ne se soumettant pas à cette loi naturelle.* Grenoble: Le Veuve Giroud, 1775.

Noiray, Jacques. "De la catastrophe à l'apaisement: l'image du fleuve de lait dans *Les Villes* et *Les Evangiles*." *Les Cahiers naturalistes* 67, 1993, 141–54.

Les Nourrices démasquées! Ce qu'elles sont en général, ce que toutes devraient être. Révélations du plus haut intérêt pour les familles, par une mère. L'époux en prescrira la lecture à sa femme. Paris: Chez Dentu, 1851.

Oppenheimer, Margaret A., "Women Artists in Paris, 1791–1814." PhD thesis. 2 vols. New York University, 1996.

Paré, Ambroise, *Deux livres de chirurgie, de la génération de l'homme, & manière d'extraire les enfans hors du ventre de la mère, ensemble ce qu'il faut faire pour la faire mieux, & plus tost accoucher, avec la cure de plusieurs maladies qui luy peuvent survenir.* Paris: Chez André Wechel, 1573. https://gallica.bnf.fr/ark:/12148/bpt6k53958h.image. Accessed December 20, 2021.

———. *Œuvres complètes.* Ed. J.-F. Malgaigne. 3 vols. Paris: J.-B. Baillière, 1840.

Pasco, Allan H. *Sick Heroes: French Society and Literature in the Romantic Age, 1750–1850.* Exeter: University of Exeter Press, 1997.

Perrottet, Tony, *Napoleon's Privates: 2,500 Years of History Unzipped.* New York: HarperCollins, 2008.

Perry, Katrina. "L'Encre et le lait: Writing the Future in Zola's *Fécondité*." *Excavatio* 13, 2001, 90–98.

Perry, Ruth. "Colonizing the Breast: Sexuality and Maternity in Eighteenth-Century England." *Journal of the History of Sexuality* 2.2, 1991, 204–34.

Petit, Léon. "La Nourrice." *Gazette de Gynécologie* 13.284 (April 15, 1898), 114–20.

Pinard, Adolphe. *De la puériculture.* Lyon: Imprimeries réunies, 1908.

Poirrier, Philippe. "Les Figures symboliques de la IIᵉ République." *Histoire par l'image.* https://histoire-image.org/fr/etudes/figures-symboliques-iie-republique?to=animation. Accessed December 20, 2021.

Pontas, Jean. *Abrégé du dictionnaire des cas de conscience de M. Pontas dans lequel on trouve un grand nombre de remarques & de nouvelles décisions.* Paris: Libraires associés, 1764.

"Prix Montyon." *Académie Française.* www.academie-francaise.fr/prix-montyon. Accessed February 27, 2020.

"Provenance de l'œuvre de Jean Goujon." *Base Joconde.* Ministère de la culture. Web. Accessed October 14, 2012.

Przybos, Julia. "Une œuvre originale? Le cas de Charlot s'amuse de Paul Bonnetain." *Australian Journal of French Studies* 42.2, 2005, 172–84.

Puzos, Nicolas. *Traité des accouchemens.* Paris: Desaint & Saillant, 1759.

Rattner Gelbart, Nina. *The King's Midwife: A History and Mystery of Madame du Coudray.* Berkeley, University of California Press, 1998.

R.E.B. "L'actualité: critique dramatique." *Le Carnet, Historique & Littéraire* 7 (January–March). Paris: Au Bureau de la Revue, 1901, 465.

"La République," Honoré Daumier. *Musée d'Orsay*. www.wikiart.org/en/honore-daumier/the-republic-1848. Accessed December 11, 2021.

Richardson, Joanna, *Victor Hugo*. New York: St. Martin's Press, 1976.

Roland, Madame Manon. *Avis à ma fille en âge et dans le cas de devenir mère*. Cited in G. Sussman, *Selling Mother's Milk: The Wet-Nursing Business in France 1715–1914*, Urbana: University of Illinois Press, 1982.

——. *Lettres de madame Roland*, vol. 1, *1780–1793*. Paris: Imprimerie Nationale, 1900–2. https://gallica.bnf.fr/ark:/12148/bpt6k46924q.image. Accessed December 20, 2021.

——. *Mémoires*. Paris: Hachette, 1864.

Roland, Jeanne-Marie. *Œuvres de J.-M. Ph. Roland, femme de l'ex-ministre de l'Intérieur, contenant: Les Mémoires et Notices Historiques qu'elle a composés dans sa prison en 1793*. 3 vols. Paris: Bidault, An VII [1798–99].

Rollet, Catherine. *La Politique à l'égard de la petite enfance sous la Troisième République*. Paris: Institut Nationale d'Études Démographiques, 1990.

——. *Les enfants au XIXe siècle*. Paris: Hachette Littératures, 2001.

Rosenblum, Robert. "Caritas Romana after 1760: Some Romantic Lactations." In Thomas B. Hess and Linda Nochlin, *Woman as Sex Object: Studies in Erotic Art, 1730–1970*. New York: Newsweek, 1972, 43–63.

Rothschild, Henri de. *Hygiène de l'allaitement: allaitement au sein, allaitement mixte, allaitement artificiel, sevrage*. Paris: Masson, 1899.

Rousseau, Jean-Jacques. *Les Confessions*. Texte de l'édition H. Launette & Cie, Paris, 1889.

——. *Correspondance complète de Jean Jacques Rousseau: édition critique étabie et annotée par R. A. Leigh*. Oxford: Voltaire Foundation, 1979.

——. *Émile, ou De l'éducation*. Paris: Garnier, 1964.

——. *Emile, or on Education*. Trans. Barbara Foxley. London: J. M. Dent and Sons, 1921.

Roze de L'Epinoy (Dr.) *Avis aux mères qui veulent allaiter, par. M. Roze de L'Epinoy, docteur-régent de la Faculté de Médecine de Paris*. Paris: Didot le jeune, 1785.

Saint-Just, Louis de. *Œuvres complètes*. Ed. Charles Vellay. Paris: Charpentier et Fasquelle, 1908.

Sand, George, *Correspondance*, édition de Georges Lubin. Paris: Classiques Garnier, 1964.

——. *Horace*. Paris: Lévy, 1857a.

——. *Isidora*. Paris: Lévy frères, 1861.

——. *Lucrezia Floriani*. Paris: Calmann-Lévy, 1880.

——. *Œuvres complètes*. 27 vols. Brussels: Méline, Cans & Cie, 1857b.

——. *Œuvres complètes*. Paris: Calmann-Lévy, 1879.

Sharp, Lynn. "Metempsychosis and Social Reform: The Individual and the Collective in Romantic Socialism." *French Historical Studies* 27.2, 2004, 349–79.

Sicard de Plauzoles, Justin-Joseph-Eugène. *La Maternité et la défense nationale contre la dépopulation*. Paris: Giard et Brière, 1909.

Simond, C. (ed.) *La vie parisienne à travers le XIXᵉ siècle: Paris de 1800 à 1900 d'après les estampes et les mémoires du temps*. Paris: Plon, 1901.

Smart, Annie. *Citoyennes: Women and the Ideal of Citizenship in Eighteenth-Century France*. Newark: University of Delaware Press, 2011.

Sperling, Jutta G. "Las Casas and His Amerindian Nurse: Tropes of Lactation in the French Colonial Imaginary (*c.*1770–1815)." *Gender & History* 23.1 (April 2011), 47–71.

Staël, Germaine Necker de. *De L'Allemagne*. Paris: Hachette, 1958–60.

———. *Lettres sur Jean-Jacques Rousseau* (1788). Geneva: Slatkine Reprints, 1979.

Stephens, Elizabeth. "Redefining Sexual Excess as a Medical Disorder: *Fin-de-siècle* Representations of Hysteria and Spermatorrhoea." In David Evans and Kate Griffiths, eds. *Pleasure and Pain in Nineteenth-Century French Literature and Culture*. Amsterdam: Rodopi, 2008, 209.

Sussman, George. *Selling Mother's Milk: The Wet-Nursing Business in France, 1715–1914*. Urbana: University of Illinois Press, 1982.

Thomas, Penrhy Vaughan. *The Plays of Eugène Brieux*. Boston: J. W. Luce & Co., 1914.

Tissot, le Dr. Samuel. *L'Onanisme: dissertation sur les maladies produites par la masturbation*. Lausanne: Chez François Grasset, 1797.

Toubin-Malinas, Catherine. *Heurs et malheurs de la femme au XIXᵉ siècle: "Fécondité" d'Émile Zola*. Paris: Klincksieck, 1986.

Toussaint, M. le Dr. E. *Hygiène de l'enfant en nourrice et au sevrage. Guide pratique de la femme qui nourrit. Par Me le Dr E. Toussaint, inspecteur du Service de protection des Enfants du premier age, Membre titulaire de la Société de médecine publique et d'hygiène professionnelle*. Paris: Doin, 1887.

'Transmigrate.' q.v. *Oxford English Dictionary*. online. www.oed.com/. Accessed April 30, 2018.

Trouillas, Paul. *Le Complexe de Marianne*. Paris: Seuil, 1988.

Trousson, Raymond. *Balzac, disciple et juge de Jean-Jacques Rousseau*. Geneva: Droz, 1983.

Vacher, F. *Solution du problème social de la surveillance des enfants en nourrice*. Lyon: Imprimerie Typo, 1873.

Valerius Maximus. *Memorable Doings and Sayings*. Trans. D. R. Shackelton Bailey. Cambridge, MA: Harvard University Press, 2000.

Van Hooff, Dominique. "Émile Zola, allaitement et fécondité." *Cahiers naturalistes* 74, 2000, 183–93.

Ventura, Gal. *Maternal Breast-Feeding and Its Substitutes in Nineteenth-Century French Art*. Leiden: Brill, 2018.

Verdier-Heurtin, Jean, *Discours et essai aphoristique sur l'allaitement et l'éducation physique des enfans, par Verdier-Heurtin, Maitre-ès-arts en la ci-devant Université; bachelier en médecine des anciennes écoles; docteur-médecin de celle de Paris … accoucheur, etc. …* Paris: L'Imprimerie d'Egron, An XII [1804].

Walker, Lesley. *A Mother's Love: Crafting Feminine Virtue in Enlightenment France*. Lewisburg, PA: Bucknell University Press, 2008.

Walwyn-Jones, J. Bonhams. Auction. Lot number 124: *La Débâcle* (Author's presentation copy). www.bonhams.com/auctions/20134/lot/124/. Accessed October 8, 2013.

Weinreb, Alice. "Red Mothers and White Milk: Maternal Lactation and American Indians in Post-Revolutionary France." *West Virginia University Philological Papers* 52, 2005, 17–23.

Witkowski, Dr. Gustave Joseph. *Tétoniana: curiosités médicales, littéraires et artistiques sur les seins et l'allaitement.* Paris: A. Maloine, 1898.

Yalom, Marilyn. *History of the Breast.* New York: Knopf, 1997.

Young, Iris Marion, *Throwing Like a Girl, and other Essays in Feminist Philosophy and Social Theory.* Bloomington: Indiana University Press, 1990.

Zola, Émile. *Correspondance.* Ed. B. H. Bakker. 11 vols. Montreal: Les Presses de l'Université de Montréal, 1983–2010.

———. "La Dépopulation." *Le Figaro* (May 23, 1896).

———. *Fécondité (Les Quatre Évangiles).* Paris: Harmattan, 1993.

———. *Germinal.* Paris: Claude Lattes, 1989.

———. "J'accuse!" *L'Aurore* (January 13, 1898), 1.

———. *Œuvres complètes,* Ed. H. Mitterrand. 21 vols. Paris: Nouveau Monde, 2002–9.

———. *Quatre Evangiles: Fécondité.* La Bibliothèque électronique du Québec. n.d. https://beq.ebooksgratuits.com/vents/zola-fecondite.pdf. Accessed December 20, 2021.

Index

Printed and bound by CPI Group (UK) Ltd, Croydon, CR0 4YY

10/12/2024